In today's culture, local gatherin
From Solomon's Temple up until
advancement of creativity and tech.
tions. Zac has created a tool to remind us, after all of our preparation,
programming, and rehearsals, of our "why." The gospel, encountering
Jesus, digging for his presence, and so much more are at the core of this
book filled with biblical and theological truths. *Before We Gather* is the
ultimate tool for your teams to sync up with before they gather together.

—GREG JOHNSON, DIRECTOR OF WORSHIP AND MEDIA,
NORTHVIEW CHRISTIAN CHURCH, DOTHAN AND
MONTGOMERY, ALABAMA, AND ATLANTA, GEORGIA

A scripturally grounded, pastorally sensitive, and theologically astute
resource for those who serve the worshiping church—all characteristics
we've come to expect from Zac's work. *The Worship Pastor* helped us understand anew the pastoral dimensions of the office of worship leader. From
this devotional reservoir, leaders are empowered to form others to lead
Christ's church with godly wisdom and Spirit-led imagination. While
there is no shortage of books supporting spiritual formation, this one
uniquely is written to worship pastors, who, alongside their teams, will
glean from it for years to come.

—EMILY SNIDER ANDREWS, EXECUTIVE DIRECTOR,
THE CENTER FOR WORSHIP AND THE ARTS; ASSISTANT
PROFESSOR OF MUSIC AND WORSHIP, SAMFORD UNIVERSITY

Worship pastors call Sunday morning "the 52 Monster"—the hungry
beast devouring our hard work and preparation every Sunday of the year.
How can we remain faithful and fruitful in such an unrelenting context?
Zac Hicks brilliantly structures *Before We Gather* as fifty-two pointers to
the person and work of the Lord Jesus, fifty-two snacks to get us through
to the final feast. It's what I need, and probably what you need as well.
Take up and read!

—MATTHEW WESTERHOLM, ASSOCIATE PROFESSOR OF CHURCH MUSIC
AND WORSHIP, THE SOUTHERN BAPTIST THEOLOGICAL SEMINARY

This grit-tested devotional tool reflects the virtues of its author. Hicks is an extraordinary blend of intellectual mind and pastoral heart. It is exciting to anticipate how God, for years to come, will use these devotions to provide purposefulness and expectancy in our gathered worship communities. Undoubtedly, they will help worship pastors, leaders, and teams embrace their roles with anointing and effectiveness.

—MIKE TAPPER, CHAIR OF RELIGION AND HUMANITIES,
SOUTHERN WESLEY UNIVERSITY

If all of worship is fundamentally our liturgical amen to the worship of Christ Jesus, then it stands to reason that our most important task is to attune ourselves to his voice, his words, his worship. This is what Zac Hicks invites readers to do in this theologically rich, biblically alert, pastorally sensitive, and immensely practical book. I hope worship teams everywhere take advantage of it to become what they hope to invite others to be: a people of prayer ravished by the beauty of God's presence and transfixed by the glory of his triune name.

—W. DAVID O. TAYLOR, ASSOCIATE PROFESSOR OF
THEOLOGY AND CULTURE, FULLER THEOLOGICAL SEMINARY;
AUTHOR, *OPEN AND UNAFRAID* AND *A BODY OF PRAISE*

This collection of devotions will help prepare the hearts and minds of all involved in leading corporate worship. Drawing from the historic practice of preparation and his devotion to discipleship, Zac Hicks has created a resource that I am sure will benefit many congregations.

—MATTHEW BOSWELL, HYMNWRITER; PASTOR, THE TRAILS
CHURCH, CELINA, TEXAS; ASSISTANT PROFESSOR OF CHURCH MUSIC
AND WORSHIP, THE SOUTHERN BAPTIST THEOLOGICAL SEMINARY

# BEFORE WE GATHER

## ALSO BY ZAC HICKS

*The Worship Pastor: A Call to Ministry for*
*Worship Leaders and Teams*

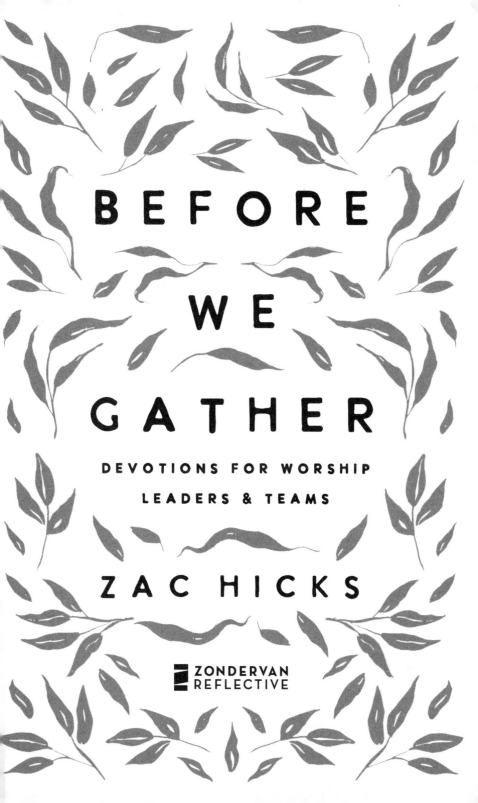

# BEFORE

# WE

# GATHER

## DEVOTIONS FOR WORSHIP
## LEADERS & TEAMS

# ZAC HICKS

ZONDERVAN
REFLECTIVE

ZONDERVAN REFLECTIVE

*Before We Gather*
Copyright © 2023 by Zachary M. Hicks

Requests for information should be addressed to:
Zondervan, *3900 Sparks Dr. SE, Grand Rapids, Michigan 49546*

Zondervan titles may be purchased in bulk for educational, business, fundraising, or sales promotional use. For information, please email SpecialMarkets@Zondervan.com.

ISBN 978-0-310-14510-3 (audio)

Library of Congress Cataloging-in-Publication Data

Names: Hicks, Zac, 1980– author.
Title: Before we gather : devotions for worship leaders and teams / Zac Hicks.
Description: Grand Rapids : Zondervan, 2023. | Includes index.
Identifiers: LCCN 2023009934 (print) | LCCN 2023009935 (ebook) | ISBN
    9780310145073 (paperback) | ISBN 9780310145097 (ebook)
Subjects: LCSH: Prayers—Christianity. | Devotional exercises. | Worship. | BISAC:
    RELIGION / Christian Rituals & Practice / Worship & Liturgy | RELIGION / Biblical
    Meditations / General
Classification: LCC BV210.3 .H529 2023 (print) | LCC BV210.3 (ebook) | DDC
    264/.13—dc23/eng/20230425
LC record available at https://lccn.loc.gov/2023009934
LC ebook record available at https://lccn.loc.gov/2023009935

Published in association with the literary agency of Wolgemuth and Associates, Inc.

*Cover design: Studio Gearbox*
*Cover photo: © Anastasiia Gevko / Shutterstock*
*Interior design: Denise Froehlich*

*Printed in the United States of America*

23  24  25  26  27   TRM   5  4  3  2  1

*To my father and mother,*
*Leon and Brenda Hicks*

*You taught me to pray and worship, and you*
*faithfully led me into Jesus' arms.*
*I love you and am forever grateful.*

# Contents

*Foreword* . . . . . . . . . . . . . . . . . . . . . . . . . . . . . . . . . . . . . . . . . xiii

Introduction. . . . . . . . . . . . . . . . . . . . . . . . . . . . . . . . . . . . .1

1. Learning How to Pray . . . . . . . . . . . . . . . . . . . . . . . .11
   *Matthew 6:7–13*

2. Bring Your Burdens On In . . . . . . . . . . . . . . . . . . 14
   *Psalm 55:22*

3. The Worship of Our Ears . . . . . . . . . . . . . . . . . . . .17
   *Psalm 40:6–8*

4. On Being a Worthy Worshiper . . . . . . . . . . . . . . . 20
   *Psalm 15:1–5*

5. Where Did You Go, God? . . . . . . . . . . . . . . . . . . . 23
   *Psalm 42*

6. Finding True Reality. . . . . . . . . . . . . . . . . . . . . . . . 26
   *Psalm 73:1–5, 13–17*

7. Worship That Makes Dead Things Alive . . . . . . . 29
   *Ezekiel 37:1–10*

8. The Living and Active Word. . . . . . . . . . . . . . . . . 32
   *Hebrews 4:12–13*

9. Worship as Wait Training. . . . . . . . . . . . . . . . . . . 35
   *Psalm 62*

10. Worshiping God versus Worshiping Worship . . . 38
    *Psalm 48*

11. Clear Glass, Not Stained Glass. . . . . . . . . . . . . . . 41
    *Numbers 21:4–9; John 3:14*

12. The Lord Is My Song . . . . . . . . . . . . . . . . . . . . . . . 44
    *Psalm 118:1–14*

13. Worshiping before the Nations . . . . . . . . . . . . . . 47
    *Psalm 108*

14. Come, Holy Spirit . . . . . . . . . . . . . . . . . . . . . . . . . 50
    *Ephesians 5:18–21*
15. The Antidote to Spiritual Amnesia. . . . . . . . . . . . 53
    *Psalm 105:1–6; 106:8–13*
16. The New Song. . . . . . . . . . . . . . . . . . . . . . . . . . . . . 56
    *Psalm 149*
17. When "Us versus Them" Becomes "We". . . . . . . . 59
    *Romans 3:9–18*
18. Our Sacrifice of Praise . . . . . . . . . . . . . . . . . . . . . 62
    *Philippians 2:1–11*
19. The Face of God . . . . . . . . . . . . . . . . . . . . . . . . . . . 65
    *Psalm 114:1–8*
20. Why Worship Isn't Always Fun . . . . . . . . . . . . . . 68
    *Psalm 119:103*
21. The Unbudding Fig Tree. . . . . . . . . . . . . . . . . . . . 72
    *Habakkuk 3:17–19*
22. The Day of the Lord . . . . . . . . . . . . . . . . . . . . . . . . 75
    *John 20:1–18*
23. Enter with Thanksgiving. . . . . . . . . . . . . . . . . . . . 78
    *Psalm 95:1–2*
24. Worship as Remembrance . . . . . . . . . . . . . . . . . . .81
    *Psalm 66:5–7*
25. The (Not So) Ordinary Work of the Holy Spirit . . 84
    *Romans 8:15–18*
26. Two More in the Battle . . . . . . . . . . . . . . . . . . . . . 87
    *Romans 8:26–27, 33–34*
27. Glory . . . . . . . . . . . . . . . . . . . . . . . . . . . . . . . . . . . . . 90
    *John 17:1–5, 20–23*
28. Worship as Confrontation . . . . . . . . . . . . . . . . . . 93
    *Psalm 115:1–8*
29. Christ Ascended . . . . . . . . . . . . . . . . . . . . . . . . . . . 96
    *Acts 1:6–11*

30. Jesus Time ............................... 99
   *John 6:41–51*
31. The Spillover ........................... 102
   *Psalm 139:1–18*
32. Always Repenting ....................... 105
   *Psalm 107:1–16, 39–43*
33. Lamentation as Praise .................... 108
   *Psalm 149*
34. The Goal of Redemption................... 111
   *Exodus 3:11–12*
35. More Than We Can See.....................114
   *Revelation 7:9–12*
36. God-Fearing.............................117
   *Psalm 34:8–14*
37. Shalom Worship ......................... 120
   *Isaiah 66:12–14*
38. Bezalel and Oholiab ......................123
   *Exodus 31:1–11*
39. Hearing Aids for the Gospel ............... 126
   *Galatians 1:3–9*
40. You're Really Getting Married.............. 129
   *Revelation 19:6–9*
41. Symbiotic Worship .......................132
   *Amos 5:18–24*
42. Beyond Us and Them .....................135
   *Psalm 139:13–23*
43. Good Old-Fashioned Submission............138
   *Psalm 2*
44. A Safe Space .............................141
   *Psalm 27:1–6*
45. Working Backward from the End ........... 144
   *Revelation 7:9–12*

46. The Wilderness of Worship ................. 147
    *Matthew 3:1–6*
47. Worshiping "Before the Gods" .............. 150
    *Psalm 138:1–6*
48. Digging for His Presence ................... 153
    *Isaiah 57:14–15*
49. Easily Blessed ........................... 156
    *1 Thessalonians 5:16–18*
50. So You Want to Encounter Jesus. ............. 159
    *Luke 24:13–32*
51. Over the Chaos. .......................... 162
    *Psalm 29*
52. What Qualifies Us to Serve ................ 165
    *Psalm 51:1–13*
    Conclusion: Passing the Baton ............. 169

*Acknowledgments* ............................. 171
*Topic Index* ................................. 173
*Bible Index* ................................. 181
*Christian Calendar Index* .................... 187
*Worship Pastor Theme Index* .................. 189

# Foreword

When I picked up this book, I was struck by its relevance. At a time when the focus of worship is often on what God can do for *us*, Zac Hicks brings us back to the heart of worship—Jesus alone. Drawing on theology and biblical truth and his experiences as a worship leader and pastor, Hicks weaves a compelling call to prioritize Jesus and his grace in our corporate worship.

Shortly after receiving the book, I devoted the beginning of our team's next rehearsal to reading one of its short devotions. As we read together, our eyes were opened to the congregation's vulnerability and the need for Jesus that each person walking through the auditorium doors would carry with them into the week. We prayed together, and I felt a new awareness—a sharper focus on the bigger picture—as we transitioned into our rehearsal. And the time we spent together also sparked me to share a moment with our congregation at our Sunday gathering later that week that allowed them to be real with God as they opened their hearts to him. A woman later told me of the emotion and gratitude toward God that welled up inside her from our time of singing. I believe the Holy Spirit worked through our Thursday night's devotion to work in the hearts of the congregation on Sunday, all for Jesus' glory. That's the beauty of *Before We Gather*.

Through a set of weekly devotions, Hicks addresses the importance of prayer and the centrality of Jesus in our worship. He challenges our assumptions about worship and speaks with a Bible-centered approach, reminding us that worship is not only about singing but concerns every part of the service.

Hicks emphasizes the importance of singing God's Word in

our worship, which has also been a key focus of CityAlight's ministry. We believe the Word of God is living and active and that singing it together embeds it in our hearts and minds. Hicks's focus on the Bible as the foundation of our worship resonates with us.

One of the most powerful aspects of this book is Hicks's ability to intertwine personal stories, real-life examples, and Bible passages to bring the message home. He shares his own struggles, such as his wife's battle with cancer, and relates them to the truths found in Scripture. He challenges us to be honest in our worship, to bring our burdens to Jesus, and to find our strength in him.

The content's authenticity left a strong impression on me. Hicks acknowledges that life is not always easy and that the members of our congregations and teams face challenges, doubts, and struggles. He addresses depression, doubt, and the feeling of God's absence. He points us back to God as the source of reality and reminds us that only God can do the work needed in our lives and in our gatherings.

*Before We Gather* challenged me as a worship leader and pastor to reevaluate my approach to worship and to refocus my heart on Jesus. Hicks reminded me of the importance of prayer, the centrality of the Word of God, and the need for dependence on the Holy Spirit. He encouraged me to be genuine in my worship, to lead with humility and grace, and to keep my eyes fixed on Jesus, the author and perfecter of our faith.

This book challenges us to refocus our hearts on Jesus and his gospel in our worship gatherings and serves as a valuable resource for worship leaders, pastors, and anyone involved in planning or participating in worship gatherings. It is a call to authenticity, prayerful dependence on God, and a vision for worship that goes beyond our experiences. I highly recommend it to anyone involved in worship ministry who wants to shape their teams and church gatherings in a way that honors God.

—Scott Lavender, CityAlight, St. Paul's
Castle Hill, Sydney, Australia

# Introduction

## THE POWER OF PRESERVICE PRAYER

Years ago, as a worship leader, I was introduced to the power of preservice prayer. But it wasn't just a free-for-all. As we gathered with our worship teams and volunteers, we prayed specific prayers. They were focused. Our prayers felt centered and filled with the Spirit because they began with the Scriptures, then burst into supplication. And I noticed a spillover effect. Not every time, but many times, you could feel the difference in the room when it came time for everyone to gather for worship. There was more energy, more life, more of an intangible vibe. Certainly, God was always there when we worshiped together. But on certain Sundays, it felt like we were quickened by the Word and by prayer to experience the power and presence of God in Christ through the Holy Spirit in a more tangible way.

In the last few churches I served, I began the practice of preservice devotions and focused prayer where there had not been something like this previously. I can tell you that nearly instantaneously, you could observe a change in the worship culture of our church. I could also tell that, incrementally, some strongholds we previously felt were impenetrable started to fall down: idols were confronted, sins were confessed, and hard hearts slowly cracked open. I guess that's what happens when you make a habit of yielding your worship services, before they start, to the Word of God and to the Holy Spirit who breathed that Word.

Evidently, God is telling the truth when he says that if we ask it will be given (Matt. 7:7). Father, forgive us for making it harder than that.

## A SURPRISING BYPRODUCT: A THEOLOGY OF WORSHIP

I also noticed something else happening. We were inadvertently, almost by osmosis, forming a theology of worship through these various passages and prayers, and we were doing it without a classroom and without a textbook (other than the Bible, of course, but it would be demeaning to call the living and active Word of God a textbook). No, these times didn't teach us everything. And yes, I still believe in the need for careful biblical and theological reflection on the event of gathered worship. Still, what we learned there, through the Word and prayer, taught us the most important things. It taught us what God cares about:

- How to approach him on his terms.
- What the purposes of gathered worship are.
- How gathered worship is connected to our whole-life worship the other six days of the week.
- How our worship connects us to the continuous stream of worship in heaven, the worship of ancient Israel, and the historic church.
- How to cherish Jesus and his gospel.
- How to identify and participate in the powerful work of the Spirit in our worship times.
- How to love others who are different from us, both while we worship and after we worship.
- How the church's worship propels us into mission and action.

Again, we didn't learn these things in a classroom with neutral-colored walls, fluorescent lights, and a smart screen. We learned them through gritty prayer in the quiet places in and around our worship space—listening to the Word, reflecting on that Word, and then praying that Word.

Over the years, I kept track of the most potent and powerful prayer times. In a way, this book is that living record of God's power, presence, and faithfulness. But it's also a tool for worship pastors, worship leaders, worship teams, and volunteers in and around the service who want to prepare their hearts together for gathered worship. This devotional will also work if you're one of these people preparing your heart alone; you should just know that these devotions speak with a communal feel. Even if you prepare by yourself—which, I must say, is wonderful and needed—my hope is that as the tractor beam of God's grace pulls you in through his Word, it also draws your heart toward others as you are drawn toward God.

##  JESUS, ONLY AND ALWAYS

This devotional is shot through with the gospel. Jesus alone, and his finished work alone, is what gets us through worship and gets us through life. We never graduate from needing this message. We all need a daily blood transfusion—a draining of self and a filling with Jesus' life. We need the gospel every day because we sin every day. So it is, then, that the gospel's proclamation in all the elements of worship is what brings the fire down. It is that word of Christ that dwells in us richly (Col. 3:16). It is that Spirit of the Anointed One, whose anointing pours down from a torn-open heaven to a torn-apart earth, drenching us in crimson grace (Mark 1:9–11). It is that boldness of our Worship Leader, who, having ripped the temple curtain in two, ushers us all into the holy of holies (Heb. 4:16; 8:1–2). Because of this gospel, this devotional won't throw us back on ourselves, or push us to do more or try harder, or feed us the lie that God is waiting to act, bless, or respond based on how devoted we are, "prayed up" we are, purely motivated we are, and sincerely surrendered we are. Rather, this devotional revels in the fact that Jesus died for all our bad worship and is the active agent in all our good worship. Its goal is to lead us into more dependence upon God, more reliance upon Jesus, and more anticipation of the Spirit's work, not ours.

### ⤳ HOW TO USE THIS BOOK

Each devotion takes approximately fifteen to twenty minutes to read, consider, and pray through. The reading portion of the entries, including the Scripture passage, is about five to eight minutes long, and the rest of the time is dedicated to focused prayer. It may not be feasible in every context to do this, but I've found great value in praying in the same room where the worship service will take place.

The devotions are broken into three sections: Scripture, devotion, and prayer.

## 1. Scripture

Because the Word of God is living and active, and because God's Word never goes out without the power and presence of the Holy Spirit, I encourage you to read the assigned passage out loud. Even if you're doing the devotion alone, it's good for your ears to physically hear the Word, and as Jesus showed us when he was tempted in the wilderness, it's always good for the enemy to hear the Word too. Pick the version or translation of the Scriptures that is most familiar in your context, though I recommend translations that stick more closely to the original text (ESV, NIV, [N]RSV, [N]KJV, NASB) than the more paraphrased versions (NLT, *The Message*). Sometimes the paraphrased versions can veer too far away from the original language, and as a result, some of the references or insights in the devotions might not make sense.

## 2. Devotion

If you're in a group, you should definitely read the devotion aloud for everyone. In the section "Customize This Book," I offer some tips on making this book your own, including both the ordering of the devotions and the language in them. Each devotion has a trajectory, though. Unlike other devotions that often lead us toward inward and personal contemplation (not a bad thing), the purpose of these devotions is to drive us into an others-focused ministry of corporate worship. You'll find that the devotions always move from reflection toward outward, kingdom-focused, and ministry-aimed prayer. That's on purpose.

## 3. Prayer

This third section of each devotion is vital. Sometimes when we turn to prayer we go into personal mode. Whether we're engaging this devotional as a group or as individual leaders, and though we don't want to bypass the real and present problems, hurts, and needs of our own lives or of the people we're praying with, we want our time in this context to be focused. We're here to pray kingdom-sized prayers for worship and the church. We have a specific job to do. So it's important that our prayers are "aimed," and to accomplish that, every devotion ends with a few bullet points that direct our attention: "This is what to pray for."

If you're using this devotional in medium or large groups gathered before the service, my advice is to encourage folks, after reading the prompts in the prayer section, to break up into groups of no more than three or four for passed-around, out-loud prayer. The smaller the groups, the more likely that everyone will have a chance to pray. You want that room filled up with the murmurs of the Spirit. You want the prayer engine of your worship space cranked and turning so that the people who enter are stepping into a worship vehicle already moving at about thirty or forty miles per hour. In my context, I often offer a final closing prayer after a few minutes of group prayer.

I'll add here, though, that there are a few staple things we should always be praying for before a worship service, and periodically it would be good to add these things to the prompts:

- *Pray for the preaching of the Word* that the preacher would be filled with the Spirit and that the people would have ears to hear as they worship through their listening and receiving.
- *Pray for the times of baptism and the Lord's Supper* that, because God reserves these as unique gifts of his presence, he would invade our lives through these ordinary practices loaded with extraordinary power.
- *Pray for the singing and praying* to be more than going through the motions, that the practices of worship wouldn't degrade into *mere* ritual but instead be filled with heart, passion, and a deep integrity.
- *Pray for the people on the margins* that children, or the disabled, or people who are new, or who might not easily feel like they fit in, or who don't yet know Jesus might find themselves addressed by God's gospel and loved by his church.
- *Pray for the clarity of the gospel* that the good news of Jesus would be the loudest and most enduring thing that everyone hears and takes away from the worship time.

## CUSTOMIZE THIS BOOK

I want this devotional to have the existential punch and immediacy that my sisters, brothers, and I felt in our preservice prayer meetings. For that reason, I admit that some of these devotions speak with a specificity that might not fit every context. For example, the devotion could refer to "this Sunday," when some of you are worshiping on a Saturday or another time of the week. Whenever this happens, change the words. Make them fit.

As I mentioned, you're free to use whatever Scripture translation best suits your context. Know that when the devotion texts quote Scripture, they're quoting the English Standard Version (ESV). Also, know that you don't have to follow the order of these devotions. You know your people. You know where they're at. Sometimes you'll need to find the right devotion for the moment. Other times I've found that without much forethought, the right devotion "found" us. Still, recognizing that there are different contexts, I've provided some indexes at the back of the book to help you organize your use of this devotional thematically.

- *Topic Index:* for connecting the devotion to certain thematic seasons. If your church organizes its worship services according to certain seasonal themes or according to the theme of the sermon or sermon series, a topic index can be useful for tethering some of the devotions to those themes. Also check out the Bible index.

- *Bible Index:* for connecting the devotion to the sermon text or the service's theme. If the topic index isn't quite hitting the mark, try using this index to find passages that either map onto or connect closely with the theme of the day. Any Scripture passage referenced or alluded to in the devotions—not just the assigned Bible reading—is included in this index.

- *Christian Calendar Index:* for connecting the devotion to the Christian year. This book is not organized around the church year, but if you serve in a context where you journey through some or all of the church seasons, such as Advent, Christmas, Epiphany, Lent, Easter, and Pentecost, this index will guide you to devotions appropriate to the church calendar. It doesn't go so far as to assign a devotion for every special day, but it will guide you to devotions that are appropriate to certain seasons. Sometimes a devotion's assignment to a season is simply because its tenor lends itself to the hues of that season (for example, waiting and longing, for Advent; penitence and heaviness, for Lent; brightness and energy, for Epiphany; power and mission, for Pentecost).

- *Worship Pastor Theme Index:* for connecting the devotion to themes outlined in *The Worship Pastor.* In a way, this book is a devotionalized form of the teachings in my previous book, *The Worship Pastor.* Many people have asked me whether *The Worship Pastor* has a devotional companion or supplementary materials—it does now! If you or your teams are working your way through that book, I highly recommend connecting this book to that journey. It will enrich and deepen your understanding and lead you to ponder and pray the concepts that you're processing. This index was designed just for that purpose.

 **FOR EVEN MORE IMPACT**

When you start going through these devotions with your teams, you just might feel the urge to cast the preservice prayer net even wider. That's a faithful urge. Not every church is ready for an all-hands-on-deck call to action, but maybe yours is. If so, don't hesitate to make this book available to your entire church community. Doing so is more feasible in smaller churches, but don't discount what God can do in a medium or large church. It could be that you and your community commit to using this book with some consistency for a year. Maybe some of you gather, while the majority of worshipers prepare individually in their homes. Maybe *everyone* gathers before the service to expectantly pray for the time of worship. (What a thought!)

 **WHAT HAPPENS AFTER THE BOOK:**
**A HOPE AND A PRAYER**

Part of the reason I wrote this book is because I've talked to enough pastors and leaders in worship ministry who have admitted to feeling underequipped to lead devotional times like these. My prayer is that this book equips leaders with not only what to lead but how to lead. And my hope is that as leaders work their way through a year's worth of Scripture, reflection, and prayer, they might gain confidence to continue this ministry in a similar manner, but borne out of their personal Scripture study and meditation. Perhaps this book can offer a Christ-centered and worship-oriented lens through which leaders can read God's Word and draw inferences and applications that bear fruit for our weekly gatherings. I invite you to join me in praying for that. So I leave you with this prayer:

*Almighty God, who alone is worthy of our worship: send your Holy Spirit to guide us to the feet of our worship leader, Jesus Christ, where we can learn from his Word how to lead and pray, that we might be fully equipped to guide others to do the same, until we are all fully formed into his likeness. Amen.*

# 1 | Learning How to Pray

 **SCRIPTURE**

*Read Matthew 6:7–13.*

 **DEVOTION**

One of the most enduring metaphors for gathered worship is this: worship is a dialogue between God and his people. God speaks, we reply. Repeat. Nearly every element of worship could fit into one of the two categories of God's revelation or our response. When you think about it, this means that a worship service is, from top to bottom, one long prayer session. We may not intuit this because it seems like only certain portions of the service are dedicated to what we formally think of as prayer (like when a minister leads us in prayer or when we all engage in a corporate prayer-reading). But if worship really is a dialogue, this means that even the elements that don't appear to be prayer are indeed prayer.

Think about it: a worship song or hymn is nothing but a corporate prayer of the people intoned with a melody. A sermon is a time when God speaks and all of us, including the preacher, listen. Communion is a time when God communicates his love to us, and we receive it. Reading Scripture is a prayerful listening to the voice of God.

We should pay attention, therefore, to that moment when Jesus taught us to pray, because when he was teaching us to pray, he was teaching us to worship. The two words "Our Father" are full of meaning for us. "Our" means that worship is a communal event, or as one pastor once said, "Worship isn't just Jesus and me, it's Jesus and we." When we are invited to address God as Father, Jesus is telling us that we can expect to experience a certain intimacy in worship—the kind of closeness a dependent child feels with a loving, tender, and available parent. And when "Our Father" is put together, Jesus is telling us that as we worship, we're worshiping alongside, even in, Jesus' own prayers as the Son of God (Heb. 2:12; Ps. 22:2), through the power of the Holy Spirit. Jesus worships *with* us, serving as our guide, our aid, even our substitute.

That the God we worship is "in heaven" tells us that when we worship, we can expect somehow to be connected to and drawn into what's happening there. Worship is what some have called a "thin place," where the membrane between the earthly and the heavenly is stretched so much that you can almost see through to the other side. We're reminded of our future and of where we're headed. We're reminded that we're caught up in the worship already happening in heaven—the praise reverberating from the angels, the saints, and even our own loved ones who have died in the Lord.

"Hallowed be thy name" clues us in that we can expect to be overwhelmed by one of God's dominant attributes—his holiness. We should anticipate encountering God to such a degree that we will feel his greatness and our smallness, his supreme worth and our unworthiness. So we can certainly expect to praise him, but we can also expect to confess to him. "Thy kingdom come, thy will be done on earth as it is in heaven" tells us that worship will shape us. It will make us future-minded people, giving us the kind of longing for God's future reign, peace, and justice that will translate into action and activity once we leave the gathering.

"Give us this day our daily bread" shows us that in worship we can expect to bring our needs and neediness, and that God will address those things in concrete and tangible ways. He will renew his promises to be faithful as our provider for each and every thing without which we can't live.

"Forgive us our trespasses" leads us to expect that God will touch us with the balm of his forgiving grace through the gospel of Jesus Christ. It pushes us to embrace the expectation that the

Holy Spirit will open up a fresh hearing for us of "Christ and him crucified" (1 Cor. 2:2). "As we forgive those who trespass against us" reveals worship's prophetic role in propelling us toward a radical reconciliation with those from whom we've been alienated. The gospel purchases for us a freedom to forgive endlessly (Matt. 18:21–22).

"Lead us not into temptation, but deliver us from evil" warns us that worship is a battlefield, because the enemy hates God's praise more than anything (Matt. 4:8–10). We can expect to be tempted away from full engagement in worship in a multitude of ways—distraction, unbelief, disunity, and arrogance.

Who knew that worship was so rich? And who knew we would encounter all this in the short prayer our Lord taught us to pray? Well, Jesus did. And it's only fitting that as we prepare to enter into this long prayer session known as gathered worship, we muster our expectations of all it can be by praying for it together.

### ⤜ PRAYER

Aim your prayers in this direction:

- Pray that all the richness and fullness of this vision of worship from the Lord's Prayer will be realized in your service today.
- If any particular aspects of worship and prayer stood out to you, pay attention to that prompting of the Holy Spirit by offering more attention in prayer about those things.
- Pray that, over the weeks, months, and years, your congregation can grow as individuals and as a body in this full-orbed vision, especially in the areas that are weak, lacking, and neglected.

# 2 | Bring Your Burdens On In

 **SCRIPTURE**

*Read Psalm 55:22.*

 **DEVOTION**

Have you ever heard someone say at the beginning of a worship service, "Leave your burdens at the door and come worship Jesus"? Friends, this is a bad idea.

In one sense, I get it. I think the intention is that we don't let life's heaviness outweigh God's worthiness to be worshiped. Still, it doesn't seem like God's heart to have you set aside a burden for an hour or so, enjoy his presence, and then pick that burden back up again at the door where you left it, as if God's waving to you on the way out saying, "Great to see you! Good luck with that!" God seems to be much more in the burden-relieving business than in the burden-pausing business.

Psalm 55:22 is a case in point. I know this reading jumped right to the end of the psalm, but spend some time later reading or praying the whole thing. There are some serious burdens being unloaded here. A lot of psalms pray about and against enemies, but only a handful identify those enemies as former close friends (vv. 13–14, 20–21).

I don't know if there's anything more burdensome, anything more disorienting, than the burden of betrayal by a loved one. "Stabbed in the back," we say. We often talk about burdens being *on* our backs. The pain of betrayal is something deeper. It's *in* our backs. What we need to remember, then, is that when the psalmist sings this worship song, he's singing it when he's at his worst. And God gives him—and us—these faithful words to sing: "Cast your burden on the LORD, and he will sustain you." There's really only one kind of worshiper out there—a burdened one. And some worshipers this Sunday will be singing when they're at their worst.

That God writes these lyrics into a public worship song tells us something about his heart for what worship really is. Worship isn't a place to set aside your burdens. Worship is a place to lay your burdens on Jesus' back and watch him do something about them. But notice the language: "Cast your burden on the LORD, and he will sustain you." It doesn't say, "He will take it for you." It doesn't say, "You'll walk away totally free of your burden." No, we get something better than the absence of our heavy burdens. We get the presence of a strong Friend who gets underneath that burden with us, who sustains us. This is what Jesus means when he offers his invitation in Matthew's gospel: "Come to me, all who labor and are heavy laden, and I will give you rest. Take my yoke upon you, and learn from me, for I am gentle and lowly in heart, and you will find rest for your souls. For my yoke is easy, and my burden is light" (Matt. 11:28–30). Jesus is saying, "When you come into my presence, when you come alongside me, the friend of sinners, you get to hitch your burdened back onto my strong back." If we go into worship feeling alone and heavy, God intends that we walk out feeling hitched to Jesus.

Have you ever seen Chick-fil-A's customer training video? Fast-food training shouldn't make you cry, but this video kind of does. It pans through a restaurant in slow motion, pausing briefly over people who are ordering food or sitting at tables. Hovering next to these people are statements like, "Lost his job this week," "Years of fighting cancer," and, "Single mom trying to make ends meet." The message is clear: everyone who walks through the door has a story. The purpose of the video is to foster in Chick-fil-A's employees an others-centered empathy so strong that it affects the way they treat the people they serve.

I wonder what it would be like for those of us who plan, lead, and facilitate worship—and for those of us who simply want to be intentional worshipers—to envision the heavy-laden nature of everyone who comes in the door. At Chick-fil-A, every customer has a story. In church, every worshiper has a burden. The good news about worship is that God's objective for this gathering is to offer the very presence of the one who, because of his life, death, and resurrection, has the power to get under every worshiper's burden in a tangible way and say, "Let me carry that with you."

Of course, we're one community. But the truth is that each worshiper has a unique burden requiring Jesus to be present to them in a specific way. That specificity is above our pay grade, though. So instead of feeling anxious that the content of this Sunday's service may or may not address exactly what people need, we go to prayer to release the burden of other people's burdens to the sovereign Spirit, who has already gone ahead of us in preparation for the service.

 **PRAYER**

Aim your prayers in this direction:

- Pray that God would draw anyone who might be trying to decide whether they will come to worship.
- Pray that people would feel free to pull down their masks, to hold their burdens up with open hands, to be honest before God and before others.
- Pray that those who are greeting and welcoming worshipers would be especially attentive and willing to drop everything to pray with someone who might need special ministry before or after the service.
- Pray that God would speak through the elements of worship with so much power and specificity that each person would find God speaking clearly and directly to them.

# 3 | The Worship of Our Ears

**SCRIPTURE**

*Read Psalm 40:6–8.*

**DEVOTION**

Because we think of gathered worship as something visibly active, we may not always clearly see how even our outwardly passive moments in worship are inwardly moments of intense activity. I'm thinking here about those moments in worship when we're seated and listening. In most worship contexts, there tend to be three kinds of these moments: (1) when someone is leading in prayer, (2) when we're hearing the Bible read, and (3) when we're listening to a sermon. Because our bodies are the least active during these moments, we can subtly buy into the idea that worshipers don't have anything to contribute here. Or worse yet, that our worship is only in the active stuff like singing or coming forward to receive communion or maybe putting money into an offering plate or basket. We stop believing that the moments of just listening aren't worship too. The Bible challenges this idea.

Psalm 40:6 carries some interesting translational baggage. Some people get concerned about that, wondering, "Well, what's the right translation? And what if we get it wrong?" Sometimes I wonder whether God doesn't give us some of these little word problems because there's something profound to discover in them. I think that's the case here. So let's follow this rabbit trail for a second. I promise there's a point.

The verse says, "In sacrifice and offering you have not delighted, but you have given me an open ear." The thrust of the Hebrew language in the second part is a little more graphic: "But you have dug out ears for me." Interestingly, some Bible manuscripts have an alternate phrase here: "But a body you have prepared for me," which the book of Hebrews picks up and interprets as coming directly from Jesus' mouth. Hebrews quotes the second rendering of Psalm 40:6 about the prepared body, rather than the first about the dug-out ear. I wonder if this isn't purposeful of God, with the dug-out-ear prayer of Psalm 40 being our prayer, and the prepared body prayer being Jesus' prayer for us.

On the one hand, our job is to recognize that God isn't after just the rituals of worship—the "sacrifices and offerings" of going through the motions of a service—he's after our hearts. One of God's primary purposes for worship is to dig out the "ears of our hearts"—to cut through all the layers of lies and distorted truth we've let cake over the entry portal for God's Word. Our social media feeds, news outlets, and binged shows have created a buildup over our hearts' sound holes, and God's living and active Word comes to us in worship to drill out once again those sonic canals. "Open up my ears so I can really worship, God." That's the prayer of the worshiper. That's our prayer.

But that leads us to the second translation of Psalm 40:6 in Hebrews 10—to Jesus' prayer for us. The dug-out ear raises the question, "What will my ear be filled with now that it's open?" And Jesus answers, "Me." When we hear Jesus pray "a body you have prepared for me," we can't help but think, based on the word "body" and the context of Hebrews 10, about the cross, the place where Jesus the Priest offered Jesus the Sacrifice for you and for me. The goal of worship according to Psalm 40:6, then, is to open our ears and then fill them with Jesus.

Martin Luther famously said, "The ear is the only organ of a Christian." What he didn't mean by this, as it applies to worship, is that there's no benefit or purpose to the other organs—our eyes, our noses, our mouths, our appendages. Without them we can't see one another's bodies, smell and taste bread and wine, and lift our hands and bend our knees. What Luther did mean is that the purpose of every organ is first and foremost one of reception. We're supposed to "hear" the gospel through all those other organs. Worship is about receiving Christ—who he is and what he has done—through all the senses.

And this ultimately means that even those visibly passive moments in worship—when someone else is praying, when someone else is reading, when someone else is preaching—aren't passive at all. Those moments are times to offer up the worship of our ears, to sit on the edge of our seats in anticipation, to wait eagerly for when the Holy Spirit will come in power and pour Jesus into the portals of our hearts. For this to happen, we need the Spirit to go before us to prepare hearts for this kind of receptivity. And so we pray.

 **PRAYER**

Aim your prayers in this direction:

- Pray for those who have allowed their sense of identity to cake over their ability to receive Christ as their identity. Pray that God would open them up again.
- Pray for the Holy Spirit to invade those who may be tempted to turn off during prayer, Scripture reading, or preaching.
- Pray for the Father to send forth his Word in the power of the Spirit, particularly to do these two things: to open up your need and receptivity, and to answer that need by filling you up with "Christ and him crucified" (1 Cor. 2:2).

# 4 | On Being a Worthy Worshiper

### SCRIPTURE

*Read Psalm 15:1–5.*

### DEVOTION

I can't tell you how many times I've been a part of prayer times before worship services when someone prayed something like this: "God we ask that you would purify our hearts and purify our motives so that we can be clean vessels for you to work through today." As the prayer goes on, it's clear that there's a logic at play: if we want the worship service to be powerful, successful, and dynamic, if we want the Spirit to come in power and move among us—move through us—we need to make sure that we are clean vessels, not dirty ones. The idea is that worshipers (and maybe especially worship leaders) are like pipelines that run from heaven to earth, and if God is going to pour out the refreshing water of his presence onto his people, those pipelines need to be free of grime, debris, corrosion, and blockage—clean vessels.

When you read a psalm like Psalm 15, you get that same impression. "Who shall sojourn in your tent? Who shall dwell on your holy hill?" It's essentially asking the question, "What kind of person is fit to worship God, to lead others in worshiping God?" And the next verse seems clear enough. It's a barrage of require-ments: You need to walk blamelessly. You need to do what is right. You need to speak truth in your heart. You need to avoid slander. You need to do no harm to your neighbor. You need to be truthful at all times. You need to be a good steward of your money. And on and on. You want worship to go well? You'd better be a clean vessel. And we shouldn't shortchange just how serious and heavy a word like this is. God is holy, after all. And we should be too (Lev. 11:44; 1 Peter 1:16).

And yet what's happening in our hearts when we receive the full force of Psalm 15? What's happening when we feel the weighty call of being a clean vessel for God to work through? I think the honest response can only be one of two things: deceit or despair. If we choose deceit, we will sugarcoat our faults, downplaying just how dire the situation is or how high the demand is. Just how clean a vessel do I need to be? Somewhat clean? Pretty clean? Am I just looking to remove the major obstructions? Is it okay to have a little grime coating the insides of the pipe as long as the water flows? That's probably good enough, right? If we take that deceptive line of thought, we dodge the absolutism of verse 2, which isn't looking for just a decently good person but one "who walks blamelessly." And so if all we've got is Psalm 15, and if self-deception isn't a real option, it appears that we're left with despair.

But (and doesn't the Bible's good news often begin with "but"?) we need to remember that the Holy Spirit, who inspired not only the content but the order of the book of Psalms, knows that Psalm 15 doesn't leave us in a hopeful place. The Spirit knows that honestly praying Psalm 15 leaves us with a huge problem. And so we are given Psalm 16, the opening lines of which pray, "Preserve me, O God, for in you I take refuge. I say to the Lord, 'You are my Lord; I have no good apart from you.'" One psalm later, one page later, a thunderbolt of grace busts a hole through what we thought was the rock bottom of our despair, tunneling a path from the Psalms straight to Jesus. Let's make the language of Psalm 16 explicit: "Preserve me, O God, for in Christ I take refuge. I say to the Lord Jesus, 'You are my Lord; I have no good apart from you, Jesus.'"

Worshipers and worship leaders must be clean vessels. And when we hide ourselves in Jesus, we are. When we give up our self-cleansing projects, when we throw ourselves on the mercy of God in Christ, we find ourselves more than ready to worship and more than ready to lead others—all because Jesus is worthy. This is what the apostle Paul meant when he said that he "put no confidence in the flesh" (Phil. 3:3). The flesh wants to own the title of clean vessel. But that glory belongs to Jesus alone, the author and perfecter of our faith (Heb. 12:2).

According to John's gospel, our job was never to be a pipeline between heaven and earth. Our job is to proclaim and receive by faith the one who is—the eternal Word who became flesh and dwelt among us (John 1:14). The good news is that we're worthy to worship today because Jesus is worthy to worship today. And funny enough, as we give up on the idea that we could ever be clean vessels, we become something God can work through. So as we go to prayer, let's commit ourselves and our fellow worshipers to making much of who Jesus is and what he has done.

###  PRAYER

Aim your prayers in this direction:

- Pray that every aspect of your worship service ultimately points to who Jesus is and what he has done.
- Pray for the Holy Spirit to come, convict, and remove from your community all confidence in the flesh.
- Pray that those who feel overwhelmed by their sin, uncleanness, shame, and unworthiness would embrace the stronger word that Jesus loves, forgives, and heals.
- Pray for your leaders in worship that they would be relieved of the burden of feeling that they need to get it all right and have it all together.

# 5 | Where Did You Go, God?

## SCRIPTURE

*Read Psalm 42.*

## DEVOTION

One of the unfortunate lies that the modern church has inadvertently spun for the watching world is that everyone who goes to church is happy all the time. Gone is the idea that we would ever come to church in sackcloth and ashes. Even if our church has a "come as you are" approach, we're still fairly put together. Somehow we're still looking good even in our casual clothes. I wonder what kind of damage we've done in the interest of making church a solely positive and happy experience? I wonder if Christians struggling with depression, doubt, and anxiety feel like worship isn't a context where that stuff gets addressed—or worse, that to struggle with those things shows that you aren't a real Christian?

God's only inspired songbook, God's original Book of Common Prayer—the book of Psalms—doesn't buy into that kind of emotional exclusion. It's shocking just how often depression and anxiety fill the language of worship in the Psalms. Psalm 42 is the classic "depression psalm." Many of us may remember old musical versions of the opening lines of this psalm set to soothing, pastoral, major-key melodies. No knock against songs like these, but I don't get the impression that Psalm 42's opening verses are sung from a calm place. It's a parched kind of thirsting. A sucking-air kind of panting. "My soul thirsts for God" strikes the person praying it as coming from a place not of victorious serenity but of defeated desperation. This hunger and this thirst exist because it feels as if God is absent, not present—far, not near. We're hungry only when we haven't eaten in a while.

The psalmist sounds like a desperate worshiper who hasn't felt God's presence for a very long time. Are you in that place? Are you straining to hang on to those feelings you once had—that nearness, that joy, that rest—that now seem so absent? Has it been a long time since you've tasted the sweetness of God's nearness in worship? The psalmist prays, through tears, "These things I remember, as I pour out my soul: how I would go with the throng and lead them in procession to the house of God with glad shouts and songs of praise" (v. 4). *I remember when things were so joyful, God. Where have those days gone? Where have you gone?*

Two things about this psalm should be a huge comfort to us and to others who are in this state. First, Psalm 42 lets us know that these feelings are normal human things to feel. The enemy wants to make us feel isolated, alone, unseen, and unknown. He'll spit the lie at us, "You're the *only* one going through this," and he'll twist that lie into our aching souls, like a corkscrew, to discourage us until we find ourselves doubting that worshiping God and being with his people have anything of value for us or even anything to say to us. Psalm 42 provides for the depressed and anxious person words not only to sing to God but to sing to God *in community* with other depressed and anxious people. What a gift!

Second, this psalm reminds us that lamentation is never the end of the journey but is, instead, a marker on the road toward a sure and good destination. Lamentation is the Holy Spirit putting despondent Christians on a path whose certain end *is* what we've been hoping for. "Why are you cast down, O my soul, and why are you in turmoil within me? Hope in God; for I shall again praise him" (v. 5).

Christians should be encouraged that lamentation in the midst of depression and anxiety is exactly what it looks like to take up their crosses (Matt. 16:24). We often think that taking up our crosses means self-sacrifice. But it also means walking through hardship just as Jesus "walked through" the cross—he endured it with hope for the joy set before him because he saw that one day, on the other side of it, was a promised resurrection, a promised new heavens and new earth. To lament is to hide ourselves in Jesus, to stand "inside" his crucifixion and cry with him, "My God, why have you forsaken me?" (Ps. 22:1; Matt. 27:46). Saying things like, "God, I need you," "God, I'm dry," "God, where are you?" is a faithful, Christian thing to do.

So if you're in that place today, know that as you come to worship, you get to join Jesus' song. Because before the Psalms were our prayers, they were Jesus' prayers. And chances are there are many more downcast people who will be walking through your church doors, gathering with you today, looking for the language of lament and hope. Pray that the Holy Spirit comes in power to groan the deeper groanings (Rom. 8:26), for their sakes, for your sake, but especially for Christ's sake.

 **PRAYER**

Aim your prayers in this direction:

- Pray that to those who come in under the weight of depression and anxiety, God would reveal himself personally and tangibly.
- Pray for those among you who are not in this place right now that God would make them sensitive to the people who are struggling and that God would draw them to minister to them, to pray for them, to reach out to them, and to care for them beyond the worship service and throughout the week.
- Pray that the Holy Spirit would prompt the folks who are struggling even to get out of bed and are on the fence about coming to worship. Pray that God would lift them and carry them to the gathering.

# 6 | Finding True Reality

### SCRIPTURE

*Read Psalm 73:1–5, 13–17.*

### DEVOTION

For the people of God, it is often the case that even just one week of living, Monday through Saturday, has the power to beat the reality out of us. Christians believe that reality is ultimately what God says. Deepest reality—the deepest truth about the way things are—isn't ultimately what others say it is or what we feel it is. It's popular these days to talk about "my reality" or "my truth," as if reality is something personal and impenetrable. God contests the idea of "my reality" and "my truth" not because he doesn't care about how we experience our lives but because if our reality isn't grounded in his, we are living in a delusion that is unhealthy for us and ultimately will be our undoing.

But again, Monday through Saturday has a way of beating reality out of us. In response to threats that squelch human flourishing, culture can't help but flip into hysterics. And this frenzied activity, peddled and chronicled on social media, reported in news cycles, and buzzed about in coffee shops, phone calls, happy hours, and office chit-chat—it all has a way of turning reality upside down. We get confused. We call good "evil," and evil "good." We lose our grip on God. *Given all this craziness, is God really real? Is God really good? Is God really as powerful as he says he is? Is God really working? I don't see it. I'm struggling to believe it.*

That doubt about God's reality can sometimes move from the cosmic to the personal. We notice the unfairness of life when we compare our experience with others'. We perceive little injustices in our own worlds. *Why is it that people doing the wrong thing seem to have all the privilege and power? Why am I, desperately trying to do the right thing, always struggling, straining, hustling, scraping? It's not fair. God, if you are who you say you are, and if reality is what you say it is, why can't I see it? Why does reality seem to contradict what you say are your ways?*

Psalm 73 is the prayer of someone who feels all of this, maybe more. In the psalm we find a bold, audacious doubter splattering all that jumbled mess of thoughts, emotions, and heartache onto the floor and saying, "See, God, look at *this!*" The psalm's complaint sounds much like what we described a second ago: "God, it seems like all the bad people, the people who don't care one bit about following your ways, have all the happiness, all the peace, all the money, all the ease, all the prosperity. I thought life in you was supposed to be a life of blessing, God! Why?" And the psalm even moves beyond complaint to despair: "All in vain have I kept my heart clean" (v. 13). "It has all been for nothing, God. Why do I even try?"

But then a crazy turning point happens. An unexpected one. The psalmist (Asaph) stops and prays: "But when I thought how to understand this, it seemed to me a wearisome task, until I went into the sanctuary of God" (vv. 16–17). His turning point came when he stopped trying to figure it out and simply went to the place of gathered worship, the place where God's Word can set right all the false realities that spin us out of control during the week.

Worship, in this light, is like a decompression chamber for human beings who have been suffocating in the atmospheric imbalances created by distorted realities. Whether it's the world perpetuating those realities (as in social media) or it's our own flesh (as in the psalmist's temptation to complain about good things happening to bad people), we have a hard time breathing in these compressed realities because our lungs were designed by our maker for a certain atmosphere—a Holy Spirit atmosphere—where

God is the air we breathe. We weren't meant to live on false realities; we were meant to live by every word that comes from the mouth of God (Matt. 4:4). The big "aha" moment of the psalm comes when the psalmist says, "My flesh and my heart may fail, but God is the strength of my heart and my portion forever" (v. 26).

Worship should be, and is, the place where true reality—the way things really are—gets reestablished. Worship is the place where God's Word is reopened, where the values of his kingdom are reasserted, where his promises of what will be are respoken, and where our orientation in and around those things is realigned. But it isn't easy or formulaic. It's hard, gritty work. It's the work of faith, prayer, and praise, all of which ultimately are gifts of God. And so we go to our knees and ask God to do what only he can do, for our own sakes and for the sakes of our brothers and sisters who will be gathering to worship with us.

##  PRAYER

Aim your prayers in this direction:

- Pray that in all the elements of worship—praying, singing, preaching, sacraments—God's Spirit would send forth his Word in such power that all our false realities would be addressed and undone and God's reality would be reestablished.
- Pray especially for individuals who are on the brink of losing control because their reality has so disoriented them. Pray that they would be addressed by God in worship and connected with another believer before they leave.

# 7 | Worship That Makes Dead Things Alive

 **SCRIPTURE**

*Read Ezekiel 37:1–10.*

 **DEVOTION**

I'm writing this on the heels of a really discouraging conversation. A friend I love has lost his faith in God—in his love, in his Word, in his existence. His arrival at this place wasn't sudden. It involved a journey of both of us watching the things he held precious get taken away. This loss includes watching what he thought his life was going to be give way over the years to what his life has become. As I listened to him, and as I ponder it now, I have nothing but empathy and sadness for him. To be honest, I'm cheating an eye upward—an accusatory side-glance to heaven: *God, where were you? God, where are you?*

I'm searching for a metaphor for what I'm feeling. I started with the picture of me standing by my friend's hospital bed, hearing the beeping of the machines that are keeping him on life support. But that metaphor doesn't go far enough. There's still a bit too much hope in a situation like that. Really, it feels like I'm standing at my friend's graveside. Past the point of hope.

A lot of people who come through the doors of the church carry dire stories in their hearts, often sealed in a chamber just under the surface. They might be like me—carrying the burden of the spiritual death of a loved one. Or they might be carrying their own deadness or the grief of a dead situation. Either way, it's a feeling of utter hopelessness. It's not 99 percent despair and 1 percent hope. It's not life support. It's death.

Sometimes we must strain through tears to remember that

God works with dead things. Dead things even seem to be God's choice creative raw materials. The prophet Ezekiel shows us this. At the end of this story stands a strong, healthy army, but the raw materials aren't wounded soldiers but bones. And the Bible wants to make it doubly clear how dead these raw materials are. These are *dry* bones. No tissue, no life, no moisture left.

So how does God do it? Well, he does it through a regular feature of a worship service: the proclamation of the Word of God. God interrogates Ezekiel, "Can these bones live?" Ezekiel's answer is funny: "O Lord God, you know." It sounds like a respectful way of saying, "Of course not! They're bones! But I'm not about to say that to *you*, because you're God." And so God tells Ezekiel to proclaim, to prophesy. And as God's Spirit moves Ezekiel to proclaim the Word of the Lord, dead things come alive.

It takes the rest of the Bible to fill out just how this moment worked. We must journey to the other end of the Scriptures to realize that any and all death-raising comes from the power of the resurrection of Jesus Christ, who is the Word of God (John 1:1) and whom Paul calls the "firstfruits" of all subsequent resurrection (1 Cor. 15:20, 23). When Ezekiel prophesied, he was ultimately preaching the gospel, the good news of Jesus Christ—who he is and what he has done. This is what hearing the Word of the Lord always ultimately means.

Worship services, at their best, are always held at gravesides. God loves camping out with his people in valleys of dry bones. Why? Because worship services are places of prophecy, Spirit-filled locations where the Word of God can be unleashed to do resurrection work. Worship songs and hymns that sing the Word and allude to the Word; prayers saturated with the Word; sermons that preach the Word; sacraments and ordinances that give the Word to our five senses—they're all, through the Spirit, packed with resurrection power.

Sometimes a service filled with that Word reminds our

despairing hopelessness that there *is* hope, even at a graveside. When we're reminded of the power of the resurrecting Word, we're filled with hope that God can take the dead things in the world and bring them to life again. And so we can turn to prayer, particularly to ask the Holy Spirit to unleash the Word to faithfully do this hope-giving, life-inspiring work. And maybe, just maybe, a resurrection will be waiting for us on the other side of our dry-boned valleys.

 **PRAYER**

Aim your prayers in this direction:

- Pray for the Holy Spirit to both "bring you out" into the valley where the deadness can be identified, and to fill all the elements of worship to proclaim the resurrecting Word.
- Pray for silent sufferers who bring their despair into the worship service undetected. Ask the Lord to minister to their pain and to open the eyes of people around them to their need.
- Pray bold prayers, asking for divine and miraculous intervention in any of the impossible dead places in your life or in the life of your church.

# 8 | The Living and Active Word

*Read Hebrews 4:12–13.*

DEVOTION

If you grew up in a church that taught you to memorize Scripture, chances are you memorized these verses. It's a provocative passage. At first blush, when we hear that God's Word is a sword, we think of it as a weapon for battle. And God's Word certainly is a battle weapon. Ephesians 6:17 says so. But the sword as a weapon for battle is not the imagery being evoked here in Hebrews. God's Word is being described as doing something different from slaying our enemies. It's slaying us.

We have to remember that the epistle to the Hebrews is uniquely interested in preaching Jesus to Hebrew people—religious people steeped in the Old Testament and acquainted with relating to God through rituals like animal sacrifice. So when the author of this letter claims that the Word of God "divides joints and marrow," we're in sacrificial territory.

The other claim being made in this passage is that the Word is "living and active." The Word itself, we could say, is a busy organism. And this is testified to all over Scripture. Psalm 147 sings that "his word runs swiftly" as God drops snow on the ground, and as he melts it (vv. 15–18). This psalm is merely relaying what we find in Genesis at creation: the Word of God does the work of God. When God *says*, "Let there be light," there's light (Gen. 1:3).

John 1 helps us understand, further, that this busy activity of the Word is the activity of Christ himself. "The Word *was* God," John declares (John 1:1). And other places like John 16 and

1 Corinthians 2 tell us that Jesus' presence in his Word's activity is specifically the presence of the Holy Spirit (John 16:8–11; 1 Cor. 2:6–16). Word-filled worship is Spirit-filled worship.

But what is the busy Word doing? The author of the letter to the Hebrews gives us the ominous picture: it's cutting us up, like a sacrifice. The author explains that the Word does this by "discerning the thoughts and intentions of the heart" (Heb. 4:12). When the Word of God is doing God's work on you in worship, you should feel an uncomfortable sense that God sees you—the real you, the true you, even the you that you tend to hide not only from others but also from yourself.

The Word does this by, in the words of Martin Luther, "calling a thing what it is." It calls our sin what it is: wrong, rebellious, and worthy of God's judgment. This kind of work is a killing kind of work. The busy Word comes at us to put our flesh to death—to take us to the end of ourselves, so that we give up all efforts to trust in ourselves not only for our salvation but for our daily walk with Jesus.

The living and active Word continually comes at us to cut us down to size and to shut down all operations that put us in the driver's seat of our faith journey. Now let's be clear: that's not good news. That's not pleasant. But it is, according to this passage, one very real way we know that God's Word is doing its work.

Thankfully, there's another activity of the Word which God intends to take place on the other side of all that destruction. Just as creation began with chaos and God spoke order, beauty, and life into it, so we too can begin to revive when we have reached the chaotic end of ourselves. And God can, and does, speak order, beauty, and life through the living and active Word about Jesus Christ—the gospel. It's why Paul says, in one of his more well-known worship passages, "Let the word of Christ dwell in you richly" as you go about the activities and rituals of worship—teaching, admonishing, singing, thanking (Col. 3:16–17).

As worshipers, then, we should have an abiding prayer and an enduring practice. Our abiding prayer should be, "God, please unleash your Word to do the work that only your Word can do: bring us to the end of ourselves and give us new life in Jesus." Our enduring practice should be to develop habits of listening for and receiving that Word's work. We should pay attention to the moments in the service—whether it's in a song, a prayer, a Scripture reading, a sermon, or when we come to the table or witness a sister's or brother's baptism—when God is saying, "I see you . . . the real you." Though it makes us squirm, we mustn't run from it. We must confess. But we should also pay attention, in all those same places, for the other Word—the Word about Christ—that has the power to take slain sacrifices like us and resurrect them into new creations.

 **PRAYER**

Aim your prayers in this direction:

- Pray boldly that in the upcoming service, God would unleash his Word to do his work of bringing you to the end of yourselves, and giving you new life in Jesus.
- Pray boldly for yourselves, and for your brothers and sisters, for open ears to hear that double-edged Word. Invite the Holy Spirit to make you receptive.
- Pray more broadly for those who plan and lead worship services, that God would be faithful to draw them, week in and week out, to saturate your worship services with the Scriptures that bring forth the living activity of the Word.

# 9 | Worship as Wait Training

## SCRIPTURE
*Read Psalm 62.*

## DEVOTION

Ambrose, a leader in the early church, is well known for calling the book of Psalms a "complete gymnasium for the soul." And for good reason. To live in the psalms—to read them, meditate on them, pray them—gives us the kind of workout that exercises all the major muscle groups of our souls. And because Psalms is a collection of worship songs specifically put together for the corporate worship of the people of God, we can say by extension that worship services should also be soul gyms for our minds, hearts, and emotions.

A particular spiritual muscle has atrophied significantly in our culture. It's the muscle of waiting. I recently caught myself having a microtantrum when I attempted to return an item I purchased online and received an automated response that someone would get back to me within forty-eight to seventy-two hours. "Forty-eight hours?" I thought. "Who waits forty-eight hours?" My hyperventilation gave way to repentance when I realized that my fast-paced, plugged-in lifestyle had conditioned me out of any ability to sit and wait.

Many of us no longer have much ability to slow down, to listen, to attend, to quiet our spirits. Push notifications and the "google-ability" of everything offer little opportunity for us to exercise our waiting muscles. As a result, we've become anemic and a bit fragile. Every small gust of suffering that blows in our direction topples us over. Our pain threshold has become very low. We lack the endurance to brace ourselves and trust when answers don't come quickly or when deliverance isn't instantaneous.

Psalm 62 is all about waiting in the midst of suffering. The psalmist feels under attack, unjustly cornered, and beaten down (vv. 3–4). Toward the end of the psalm, some liabilities of impatience are exposed as the weary psalmist warns against extortion, robbery, and setting our hearts on riches (v. 10). Weak waiting muscles often make us flee to other safeties—vain attempts to self-therapize away the discomfort, exposure, and vulnerability we feel in the waiting. We seek refuge in wealth, or security in extracting what we think we can get from others.

As a worship song, Psalm 62 teaches us that our weekly gathering is a context for countercultural "wait training." It's a place of pausing where we can cut ourselves off from our devices for an hour or so. It's a place of quiet where we can wait in silence. It's a place of praise that helps us remember we worship a God big enough to trust. It's a place of relief where we release control of our schedules, our emotions, and our lives. It's a place of surrender where we submit to letting God and his Word do the leading. It's a place of hope where we are repointed to the promised coming of the King and his kingdom.

Worship also, as it proclaims the gospel of Jesus, mirrors Psalm 62's emphasis on the singularity, the "aloneness," of the object of our waiting. What are we waiting for? The psalm answers, "For God alone my soul waits. . . . He alone is my rock" (vv. 1–2). So as we proclaim and rehearse the gospel that Jesus alone is our hope and that our best efforts are filthy rags, we exercise the muscles of releasing control, letting go, practicing patience, and embracing dependency. We learn that trust and patience are closely related: because God is faithful (trust), I can wait (patience).

Perhaps today you or your brothers and sisters are coming to worship with unanswered prayers and questions. Maybe someone got a diagnosis late last week, but the follow-up got pushed to later this week. Maybe a young wife is struggling with infertility, or a single man just wants to be married and start a family. Maybe someone has been job hunting for way too long. Maybe a couple is waiting for their marriage to heal. Maybe someone with a disability or chronic illness is at the end of their rope. Pray that today's worship service would be a place where all these kinds of waiting can find a God big enough to trust, loving enough to lean on, and mighty enough to deliver. Pray that the muscles of waiting would find opportunities to stretch and flex. Pray that the elements of worship train people in the exercise of hope.

### ⤳ PRAYER

Aim your prayers in this direction:

- Pray that the worship service today would be a training ground for brothers and sisters who need to grow in waiting on the Lord.
- Pray especially for those whose waiting may be reaching a breaking point, that the service might be God's vehicle to relieve them from their burdens, strengthen them by bearing their burdens with them, or fortify them with fresh patience to press on in faithfulness.
- Pray that people would give themselves over to full-hearted, full-bodied participation in all the elements of worship for the sake of maximizing their training and formation into the likeness of Jesus.
- Pray that the gospel would be so clear and powerful that waiting gets transformed from fearful uncertainty to confident dependence.

# 10 | Worshiping God versus Worshiping Worship

**SCRIPTURE**

*Read Psalm 48.*

**DEVOTION**

Though we don't want to carry with us a destructively low self-esteem, there's a blessed realism in memorizing a Bible verse like Jeremiah 17:9: "The heart is deceitful above all things, and desperately sick; who can understand it?" I find myself going back to this verse weekly, if not daily.

Our hearts tend to take good things and turn them into self-destructive things. We could cite example after example, both in Scripture and in modern culture, of this propensity to weaponize good gifts and transfigure them into idols. One of the things we always need to be on the lookout for is how our hearts can shift from worshiping God to worshiping worship, turning the vehicle for worship into the object of worship, making the means the end.

Psalm 48 shows us one of the heart's methods for turning the worship of God into the worship of worship: when we turn the things in and around our worship services into things we need for worship. The psalm makes it clear that God is not opposed to the "stuff." The psalm's lyrics are full of admiration for the physical place of worship—Mount Zion (v. 2), her citadels (vv. 3, 13), the city (v. 8), the temple (v. 9), and the city's towers and ramparts (vv. 12–13).

But Psalm 48 makes a huge claim that we shouldn't miss: it's a check on all the admiration of the "stuff." Verse 3 establishes that as worshipers ponder and inspect the city, her temple, and her protective walls, God "has made *himself* known as a fortress."

The physical fortress must never be a substitute refuge for the real fortress, which is God alone. Israel was always in danger of putting their trust—their sense of security, stability, yes, salvation—in the things they could see rather than in the God to whom those things pointed.

In worship, God gives us many means and media to assist us in the divine encounter. Certainly, God has ordained talented human beings to communicate his Word to us in preaching. Certainly, God has given us signs and seals of his grace: bread and wine at the table and water at baptism. Certainly, God has given us musical instruments to accompany our voices (Psalm 150). Certainly, he has placed many of us in buildings outfitted with technologies that enhance the beauty and apprehension of his presence—sound systems, lighting, furniture, screens, decorations, and other art. And all those things contribute to our ability to feel and enjoy God's presence. But we're in perilous territory when we move from loving God in worship to loving the feelings that we get in worship.

God wants to use all those things to make himself known as the true object of worship, just as he intended that Israel would recognize Zion's citadels as concrete symbols and reminders that he alone is the one keeping them safe. It's one thing to appreciate a great preacher, but it's another thing to depend on that person's ability and charisma for being able to hear God in a sermon. It's one thing to thank God for great musicians; it's another thing to feel like we haven't worshiped if the music or song selections weren't right. It's one thing for your room's ambiance to lead you to feelings of awe and transcendence before God; it's another to feel like you need a worship space like that to encounter God.

Just because it's God's gentle lovingkindness, not his cold austerity, that leads us to repentance (Rom. 2:4), we shouldn't think that God wants us to whitewash our walls and do away with all of worship's "stuff." Our hearts will just find other things to latch on to in their place. Instead, our response to the revelation of Psalm 48 can be twofold: First, we can simply give God thanks for his good and faithful gifts—for the technology, the talent, and all the manifold means of grace. Second, we can walk in perpetual repentance, asking God to purify our worship through Jesus Christ, who alone worshiped the Father with singlehearted affection. Jesus intercedes for us, then invites us to approach God's throne boldly (Heb. 4:14–16).

 **PRAYER**

Aim your prayers in this direction:

- Pray for yourselves and your entire church community, that you would never mistake the "stuff" of worship for God himself, and that God would continue to purify your hearts and motives about why we worship and whom we worship.
- Pray that the various aspects of worship—from the room to the aesthetic environment, from the leaders up front to the music and content of the service—would all ultimately "get out of the way" and point people's hearts toward seeing and savoring Jesus Christ.
- Pray that the Holy Spirit would amplify and magnify our apprehension of Jesus' glory—particularly his glory on the cross—so that Jesus might be more beautiful and believable today than yesterday.

# 11 | Clear Glass, Not Stained Glass

## SCRIPTURE

*Read Numbers 21:4–9; John 3:14.*

## DEVOTION

In another devotion, we contrasted the subtle yet cosmic difference between worshiping God versus worshiping worship. Today's devotion is another way of looking at the same issue. What we want to say, right at the beginning, is that God intends everything that happens in worship to be transparent. God has a goal in worship. That goal is to draw all of creation back into the joyful bliss of his glory though union and communion with him.

In the book of Numbers, Moses recounts a harrowing episode in the middle of God's deliverance process. The Israelites had yet again grown "impatient on the way" (Num. 21:4). They grumbled and complained, once again revealing their lack of faith in God and trust in his promises to provide, protect, and deliver. Their faithlessness was met with a severe mercy (loving discipline) intended to soften their hard hearts and press them back into dependence on God. So the Lord sent serpents. But just as God's law is always accompanied by his gospel, just as his judgment is intended to lead us to his grace, so God provides a way out. Moses was instructed to fashion an artifact—a bronze snake on a pole—to serve as a "transparent" means through which God's people could receive healing and salvation. And it worked.

Generations later, though, in a little throwaway line in the book of 2 Kings, we see what happened over time to the bronze snake. What was once a means of God's saving work, what was once a vehicle for worship, became an object of worship. The text tells us that King Hezekiah "broke in pieces the bronze serpent that Moses had made, for until those days the people of Israel had made offerings to it (it was called Nehushtan)" (2 Kings 18:4). Somewhere along the way, Israel stopped looking *through* the bronze snake to God the Healer and Redeemer, and they started looking *at* the bronze snake as their healer and redeemer. The snake ceased to be transparent.

There's a helpful analogy here as we transfer these thoughts to our worship gatherings: worship should be "clear glass, not stained glass." Think about the function of each type of glass. A clear glass window is intended to be looked through. A stained glass window is intended to be looked at. A clear glass window channels light so we might see more clearly what is beyond it. A stained glass window harnesses light to magnify itself. (And by the way, this isn't a knock against stained glass windows. We're playing in the land of metaphor!) Just like the bronze snake, it's dangerous when the vehicles for worship become objects of worship.

Where are the dangers in our worshiping community? What are the sacred cows of our worship services? Is it the music? Is it the liturgy? Is it the actions and behaviors of the ministers and worship leaders? Is it the artful delivery of the preacher? Is it the beauty of our building or the sophistication of our technology? A good litmus test here is asking the question, What are people saying when they walk out of the service? "Wow, that preacher really can preach!" or "Isn't the liturgy just beautiful?" or "Wasn't the choir's anthem magnificent?" or "Isn't our worship band the best?" Ultimately, we hope people are saying none of these things. If the elements of our worship services are transparent, people walking out of a service will be exclaiming, "Isn't Jesus beautiful? Hallelujah, what a Savior!" Clear glass, not stained glass.

And what are we ultimately looking at through the clear glass? Where should all this point? Jesus tells us in a clandestine meeting with an Old Testament scholar. Jesus declared to Nicodemus,

"As Moses lifted up the serpent in the wilderness, so must the Son of Man be lifted up" (John 3:14). To "lift up" is certainly a worship phrase, but in John it has a specific meaning. Jesus was foreshadowing that moment when he would be lifted up on the cross for the sins of the world (John 8:28; 19:16–30). Just as every book of the Bible ultimately leads us to the cross, so every element of worship should do the same. The only thing beyond the clear glass is a view to Calvary's hill. So today, as we turn to prayer, we aim all our sights on that goal.

 **PRAYER**

Aim your prayers in this direction:

- Pray that every aspect of worship—the music, the technology, the prayers, the architecture, the accoutrements, the leadership—would be clear glass through which everyone will see Jesus high and lifted up.
- Pray for the Holy Spirit to graciously identify those things in your worship life and in your church's worship life that have become stained glass, that he might lead you to greater dependence on and trust in God alone.
- Pray for the people in and around the worship experience— those welcoming and greeting, those with specific duties of worship preparation and maintenance—to be used by God to till the soil of people's hearts to be ready for the Spirit to sow the seeds of the gospel in them throughout the worship service.

# 12 | The Lord Is My Song

SCRIPTURE

*Read Psalm 118:1–14.*

DEVOTION

Some days, it's really hard to sing. Singing demands so much from you. Done properly, it's one of the few modes of human expression that requires so much of your faculties—mind, body, spirit, will, and emotions. It's taxing. No wonder God wants us to sing to him! As an art form, singing just might be the clearest symbol of whole-life worship—offering our entire selves as living sacrifices to God (Rom. 12:1).

Singing is also an exercise in vulnerability. When I sing, you're not just hearing an instrument that someone made, you're hearing *me*. It's like allowing the inmost portion of your soul to expose itself to others. For these reasons and more, singing is hard enough to do on the good days. For many people, it just might be impossible on the bad days.

It might be hard to admit, but have you ever come to worship and felt like you really didn't want to sing that day? Did it feel like it would take more energy or joy than you had, or like you'd be an impostor because your heart wouldn't really be in it?

Funny enough, if you really think about the lyrics to Psalm 118, you get the impression that it's a song written by someone who's really struggling to sing. On one read, perhaps you could hear phrases like "the Lord is on my side; I will not fear" (v. 6) as bold, triumphant, and joyful. But if you pay attention to the feeling words the psalmist uses throughout, you get the impression that he's trying to convince himself that all these triumphant truths are real and worth singing about. The psalmist says he is in "distress" (v. 5), that he's "surrounded" (vv. 10–12), and that he's "falling" (v. 13).

I don't know about you, but when I'm feeling those things, the last thing I want to do is sing.

So why is the psalmist singing? What gives him the strength? Verse 14 is the answer: "The Lord is my strength and my song." Surprise! The psalmist isn't singing at all. The Lord is.

When the psalmist sings "the Lord is my song," it's not only that the Lord is the content of his song. Nor is it merely some symbolic way of saying that God is the object or audience of his song. The Lord himself is his song. When we sing, therefore, we don't just sing about the Lord or to the Lord. When we sing, the Lord himself sings.

Scripture attests that God is a singer. Zephaniah 3:17 says that God "is in your midst, a mighty one who will save; he will rejoice over you with gladness; he will quiet you by his love; he will exult over you with loud singing." And not only is God a singer, but God the Son is said to be singing with us when we gather for worship. Quoting Psalm 22, Hebrews 2:12 has Jesus declaring, "I will tell of your name to my brothers; in the midst of the congregation I will sing your praise."

And right here, we're able to make a connection between our singing Savior and what it means when Scripture says that, as the church, we are the "body of Christ" (Rom. 12:5; 1 Cor. 12:12, 27; Eph. 4:12; Col. 3:15). The body of Christ is more than a metaphor. And if so, it means that when the body of Christ sings, the voice of Christ's singing can be heard.

If that's not encouraging enough for weary singers, listen to the whole verse: "the Lord is my strength and my song; he has become my salvation" (Ps. 118:14). It makes a connection between singing and strengthening. When we sing (really, as Jesus sings), we're buoyed, lifted up. And another connection is made, as well—salvation. The song Jesus sings is his song of salvation—the anthem of the cross, where Jesus loved us and gave himself for us (Gal. 2:20). When Jesus gave himself for us, evidently that included both his song and his singing.

This is all around good news any way you look at it. If you don't have the strength to sing, Jesus will sing for you. If you're able to sing, Jesus is the one singing in you and alongside of you. So get ready, your strength is coming. You're going to hear his voice today, and it's going to sound a lot like love, mercy, and grace.

 **PRAYER**

Aim your prayers in this direction:

- Pray that the Holy Spirit fills your church this morning with an inspiring and powerful voice.
- Pray that timid singers would find themselves strengthened and confident to sing out, and that people who are too weary to sing wouldn't be embarrassed but feel the freedom to simply soak in Jesus' song.
- Pray for all the musicians who will lead the singing today—that their musicianship would be skilled, beautiful, and inspiring, and that they would be able not just to accompany the church's song but also to join it.

# 13 | Worshiping before the Nations

**SCRIPTURE**

*Read Psalm 108.*

**DEVOTION**

We always need to avoid the temptation to see gathered worship as an escape from the world. To be sure, worship is a place where the membrane between earth and heaven grows very thin; God does give us unique gifts of his presence and future kingdom here. To be sure, worship is a place to find God's stillness and peace amid lives that are chaotic and confusing. But the Bible reminds us that the whole world isn't irrelevant to worship. Instead, worship brings it into focus.

Psalm 108 is one of those "missionary" worship songs that bring the world into focus. It begins with the songwriter's enthusiasm for gathered worship. He's so anxious to worship, he has to go wake up the instruments that they will use—"Awake, O harp and lyre!"—and he even has to go wake up the sunrise while it's still dark—"I will awake the dawn!" (v. 2). The psalmist is so eager to worship, it's almost like he can't even wait for God's timing to do it. "Let's get started now! Wake up, everybody!" he shouts.

His enthusiasm is all the more surprising when we realize that he's not writing this worship song out of a place of rest and peace. The end of the psalm might seem surprising to us, but verses 10 through 13 make it clear that he's in the midst of battle with his enemies and living in the tension of God's promises unrealized. He feels full-blown rejected by God because it doesn't seem like God is with them in battle (vv. 11–12). There's something remarkable and worth emulating about a person who is filled with anxiety and doubt expressing such eagerness to gather for worship. *O God, make us that kind of worshiper!* But as we said, the world is in focus in this psalm, and therefore we get a glimpse into the Bible's connection between gathered worship and our mission to the world.

First, we recognize that worship is always to be done "among the nations" and "among the peoples" (v. 3). Throughout biblical history, God always had in mind gathering the nations. Way back in the beginning of God's salvation plan, when he singled out Abraham, his purpose was clear. Abraham's family was called out not only so that they could be a nation holy unto the Lord but also so that "all the families of the earth shall be blessed" (Gen. 12:3). Flip over to the other end of the Bible and you find the apostle Paul admonishing the young church in Corinth to keep in mind the "outsiders and unbelievers" as they worship together (1 Cor. 14:20–25). It's passages like these that have instilled in Christians the practice of inviting their non-Christian friends and family members to worship services. Worshiping "among the nations" is part of God's design for us.

Second, worship fuels a passion for God's mission to the world. If we really are encountering God's glory in worship (and know that *glory* is a big worship word that spans all of Scripture), then the natural byproduct is that we'll join the psalmist's eager desire to "let your glory be over all the earth!" (v. 5). In effect, we're saying, "God, I see how amazing you are, how gracious you are, how wonderful you are, and I want the whole world to see what I see and to know what I know!" A yearning for others to know the Lord is the fruit of having met with him yourself. So we should expect that worship should end with a propulsive effect. We should feel a holy wind at our backs, pushing us into the world to live out our vocations and continue worshiping and testifying "among the nations."

Third, worship doesn't sugarcoat the problems with the world. That the psalm ends with the songwriter's angst about God's unfulfilled promises, with his enemies remaining rebellious and unconquered, reminds us that part of our mission to the world is to desire the same submission to God "out there" as "in here." Worship creates a longing for God's vindication of wrongs and a quelling of rebellion. It stokes the fires of God's justice that his kingdom would be realized not only in the worship service but everywhere. Where is there room for our churches and our hearts to go farther here? Where might the gospel yet do more work among us and in the world for the sake of God's glory and Christ's redemption? Along with the psalmist, we go to prayer asking these questions and pleading for God's help.

 **PRAYER**

Aim your prayers in this direction:

- Pray for all who do not yet know Jesus, who may show up in your worship service. Pray that the gospel would be proclaimed clearly and that the Spirit would give all who attend ears to hear.
- Pray that God would stir up a passion for mission in your church.
- Pray that your worship service would be a context where your church is formed into a missionary people.
- Pray that God would pull people out of their comfort zones today, especially so that outsiders might feel welcomed, loved, and seen. Ask God to give a special measure of grace to those on the front lines of welcoming people to give them eyes to see and a sense of who might be most in need of special attention today.

# 14 | Come, Holy Spirit

**SCRIPTURE**

*Read Ephesians 5:18–21.*

**DEVOTION**

The question sometimes gets asked, "If the Holy Spirit is present everywhere, why do some Christians pray and sing to invite the Holy Spirit's presence among them in worship?" Why would we ask God to be where he already is?

There's good reason why for centuries Christians have been inviting the Holy Spirit to be among them. It's an ancient worship practice called invocation. The early church often invoked the presence of the Holy Spirit before ordaining a minister. The Reformation church invoked the Spirit before the reading and preaching of the Scriptures. Eastern Orthodox Christians invoke the Holy Spirit during communion. And Pentecostal Christians invoke the Spirit for singing.

And they're all right.

The evidence of the Bible around all these practices tells us that God's special presence comes as we do these things (Matt. 3:13–17; Ezek. 37:1–10; Luke 24:30–32; Eph. 5:18–21). But that still doesn't answer our question. What are we doing when we ask an omnipresent Spirit to be present among us, to visit us, or to "come and fill this place"?

Ephesians 5 helps us. The Scriptures make it clear elsewhere that we can't flee anywhere that the Spirit is not (Ps. 139:7–12). But here in Ephesians, we hear the apostle Paul commanding the Ephesian Christians, who are already filled with the Holy Spirit, to "be filled with the Spirit" (v. 18). The Scriptures teach clearly that when repentant sinners come to faith, they are immediately indwelled by the Holy Spirit (Acts 2:38–39; 1 Cor. 12:13; Rom. 8:9; Eph. 1:13–14). But when Paul commands us to "be filled," he is talking about something different. Beyond the permanent presence of the Holy Spirit, to "be filled" with the Spirit is to receive a unique manifestation of his presence and power.

Though we're not quite sure how it all works—nor do we need to be sure—we know enough to say that the Spirit, who is always present, becomes more tangible to us. Our eyes are more open to and aware of his movements for specific purposes. When the Spirit comes in special and powerful ways, we could say that the Spirit's presence, which is always there, is manifested uniquely and our spiritual senses are quickened to notice it.

In Ephesians 5, we see that the Spirit manifests himself for specific purposes in the worshiping assembly, evidenced in all those "ing" verbs—addressing, singing, making melody, giving thanks, and submitting (vv. 19–21). So in worship, we should be on the lookout for the Spirit's unique work in all these things, among the other things we've already mentioned, such as preaching and communion, and even baptism.

We shouldn't shy away from this strange and wonderful Christian practice of invocation. And here's the payoff: When the Spirit comes and makes himself tangible to us, we can be sure that he comes to do everything the Scriptures tell us is true about him. The Spirit comes to help us understand the Word of God (John 16:13). The Spirit comes to lead us into confession by convicting us of our sin and need for Jesus (John 16:8). The Spirit comes to apply Jesus to our wounds and make him more beautiful and believable to us than we ever could have imagined (Matt. 3:16–17). The Spirit comes to help us feel the Father's pleasure in the Son (Mark 1:11). The Spirit comes to help us fearlessly pray to God (Rom. 8:15). And when we don't know how to pray, the Spirit comes to pray for us (Rom. 8:26). The Spirit comes to remind us of our identity as adopted daughters and sons (Rom. 8:15–17). The Spirit comes to remind us that we have a promised resurrection, eternal life, in Jesus (Rom. 8:11).

With all these benefits and promises, what can we do but come with joy and expectation? So by all means, ask, seek, and knock. Pray to the Spirit and hold him to his word and promises. Ask him to come. And then watch out!

### ◁| PRAYER

Aim your prayers in this direction:

- Pray multiple prayers of invocation over your worship time today. Ask specifically for the Holy Spirit to come and do the various things we've listed.
- Pray for worshipers, as well, to be prepared, attuned, and ready to encounter and respond to the presence and power of the Spirit.

# 15 | The Antidote to Spiritual Amnesia

 **SCRIPTURE**

*Read Psalms 105:1–6; 106:8–13.*

 **DEVOTION**

Medical science tells story after story of trauma victims who suffer from amnesia—the inability to remember. Sometimes the trauma is physical. A blow to the head can result in short- or long-term memory loss. Sometimes the trauma is emotional and psychological. To avoid crippling psychological pain, victims of abuse can lock up significant memories in forgotten chambers of their brains and hearts.

A similar dynamic is at play for Christians when it comes to accepting the truth of their ongoing condition (Rom. 7:19–21; Gal. 5:16–17). A Christian is someone who has been quickened by the Holy Spirit and awakened, therefore, to the truth: the truth of who God is as sole creator, sustainer, and redeemer; and the truth of who we are as helpless, aimless sinners apart from his grace. That second truth—the truth of who we are—is a truth that humanity has been avoiding since our first ancestors walked the earth (Gen. 3:8). It's not easy to hear that we are defenseless, dependent creatures. In fact, it's downright traumatic.

And so, even as Christians who have tasted and seen that the Lord is good, we develop defense mechanisms, including a kind of spiritual amnesia. On a daily basis, our three enemies—the world, the flesh, and the devil—combine forces to help us forget who we really are. The world and the devil tell our flesh the lies it wants to hear: "You're growing stronger. You're less dependent. You can stand on your own two feet. Things aren't so bad."

Spiritual amnesia is forgetting that we were created as dependent creatures, and that we were redeemed back into the freedom of that dependence. And this is where worship comes in. Worship exists to retell the sacred stories that our fleshly amnesia is always trying to forget.

The book of Psalms is designed to help us remember. It is divided into five books—five subcollections to mirror the five books of Moses, as if to say, "If you sing and pray these words, you sing and pray the whole story." It's not insignificant that at the close of the fourth book, Psalms 105 and 106 retell and respond to the stories of redemption.

Psalm 105 opens by commanding us to come to worship and "give thanks to the LORD" and to "make known his deeds among the peoples." Then it walks through the story of those deeds: Abraham the wanderer, protected by God (vv. 12–15); Joseph the slave, positioned to save Israel from famine (vv. 16–22); and Moses the liberator, raised up to lead Israel out of slavery (vv. 26–45).

It's funny, though. Turn the page over to Psalm 106 and, after being summoned to praise once again, you're immediately thrust into one long confession, which basically goes like this: God did all these wonderful things, "but they soon forgot his works" (v. 13); "they forgot God, their Savior, who had done great things in Egypt" (v. 21). It's clear from the juxtaposition of these two worship songs—Psalms 105 and 106—that spiritual amnesia is a real thing. A daily thing.

Our worship services, therefore, must be places where our amnesia is confronted—where the truth-stories of our spiritual poverty and God's redemptive riches are told and retold, and where we freshly confess and freshly hear the good news.

Some Christians have asked over the generations, "Why do we need to confess our sins in worship? Doesn't the Bible teach that Jesus dealt with all our sins once for all on the cross?" The issue isn't about the scope of Jesus' full and final work. That's settled forever and ever, amen. The issue is that our flesh hates to remember its dependence. The issue is that we are prone to forget that story. So worship must tell it again and again. And we must confess it again and again.

### ◁ PRAYER

Aim your prayers in this direction:

- Pray for real moments of confrontation and grace to take place in the worship service.
- Pray that worship would feel like a safe place to be real before the Lord.
- Pray that the Holy Spirit would awaken people to the way things are and cut through the fog of spiritual amnesia.
- Pray for the clarity and power of the good news of the gospel to cut through all the other messages that we tend to hear and be distracted by.

# 16 | The New Song

 SCRIPTURE

*Read Psalm 149.*

DEVOTION

Scripture mentions singing a "new song" nine times. Five times, we are commanded to sing a new song (Pss. 33:3; 96:1; 98:1; 149:1; Isa. 42:10). Two times, the heavens are peeled back and the apostle John hears singing around God's throne—a new song, an eternal song to Jesus, the Lamb who was slain (Rev. 5:9; 14:3). One time, the psalmist declares "I will sing a new song" as if it describes an act of the will in the face of suffering and opposition (Ps. 144:9). The final time is not something that we do for God but something that God does to us when he saves us: he puts a new song in our mouths (Ps. 40:3).

This ninefold scriptural witness gives us the strong impression that singing is really important. Singing is, in fact, eternal. Over the ages, the church has interpreted the idea of the new song with a wonderful and complementary variety, and those interpretations generally offer us three insights: first, we should sing new songs; second, we should sing old songs newly; third, singing new songs will be an eternal reality.

So first: singing new songs. It's telling that the command to sing new songs is peppered throughout God's only inspired songbook, the Psalms. It's even more telling that at the end of the Psalms, in Psalm 149, the command is repeated, as if God is saying, "I've given you my songs; now continue what I've started. Write more." Over the years, I've reflected as a pastor on just why it's so important for churches to consistently incorporate new material and not merely recycle the old. New songs stoke a fire that tends always to grow cold. New songs are like new logs on a well-burning fire. They ensure the fire will keep on burning. God has wired us to be stirred by new sounds, new melodies, and new texts.

The command to sing new songs is a charge to the songwriters and poets in a congregation. Sure, the pastors, worship leaders, and music directors can find new songs from all the wonderful offerings being produced out there in Christ's church—and we should. But there's also a blessing in a church's hearing from *its* pastors and *its* poets. Who best knows the hearts of the people? Who best knows just what song needs to be sung in this moment? The church's own leaders! So go for it, leaders. The Spirit is with you.

Second: singing old songs newly. Some have rightly pointed out that replacing old songs with new songs isn't the only way to be faithful to the new-song command. Sometimes the same logs just need to be stirred a little bit. Sometimes old songs take on new meanings in present circumstances. When my wife battled eye cancer and lost vision in her left eye, the ancient hymn "Be Thou My Vision" took on a whole new meaning for her, and believe me, it was a new song. Old songs can be sung newly because we never approach them from the same place. Life is evolutionary. We change; circumstances change. We grow; we shrivel. Some parts of us die. New parts of us spring forth. And all those changes mean that sometimes a new song is simply a song we've always sung, except now we are singing it in a new place. So let's keep singing those time-tested, faithful songs that the church has sung for generations.

Third: the new song as an eternal reality. Whether we're singing brand-new songs or old songs newly, doing both of these things trains us for eternity. The apostle John, who wrote the book of Revelation, was aware of the language of the Psalms when it came to "new song," and he therefore used that phrase to describe what he heard in heaven. When he heard the song to Jesus in Revelation 5, "Worthy are you to take the scroll . . . for you were slain, and by your blood you ransomed people for God from every tribe and language and people and nation," he described it as a new song (Rev. 5:9–10). It's as if he's pointing out that the new song heralded in the Psalms and Isaiah drives toward the eternal song to Jesus. All new songs we sing are cosmically wrapped up in the heavenly Jesus song, surrounding that master song with thousands upon thousands of other overtures, other new songs.

As we sing to the Lord a new song, we train our muscles—our spiritual ones *and* our physical ones (because, don't forget, we'll have bodies on the other side of all of this)—for our eternal existence. Sing boldly. Sing newly. Sing eternally. As we go to the Lord in prayer, aiming our sights today particularly on the sung portion of our worship services, let's ask the Holy Spirit to fill our music with all kinds of new presence and power (Eph. 5:18–19).

 **PRAYER**

Aim your prayers in this direction:

- Pray that the Holy Spirit would stir the flames of newness in the old songs that you sing.
- Pray that the Holy Spirit would raise up fresh songs from and for your local body.
- Pray specifically for people who don't sing, don't see the value in singing, or feel hindered from singing—because they think they have a bad voice or because they're suffering or because they're simply making poor excuses. Pray that the Spirit would tenderly meet them and embolden them to receive the blessing of singing out.

# 17 | When "Us versus Them" Becomes "We"

## SCRIPTURE

*Read Romans 3:9–18.*

## DEVOTION

This section of Romans isn't at all the kind of pick-me-up passage we associate with warm devotions. We're jumping, midstream, into the deepest and darkest part of the river of Paul's careful articulation of the gospel to the church in Rome. The brilliance of the good news of Jesus will always shine brightest against the dark backdrop of our sin. And we just read the darkest part.

What in the world does this darkness have to do with worship?

Sometimes paying attention to those little footnotes in our Bibles pays off, and this is one of those times. As Paul is laying out this bleak picture of sin, our footnotes tell us that he's stringing together quotations largely from the Psalms. He's playing clips from God's worship songs.

- "None is righteous, no, not one" (Rom. 3:10). That's from Psalms 14 and 53.
- "Their throat is an open grave" (v. 13). That's from Psalm 5.
- "The venom of asps is under their lips" (v. 13). That's from Psalm 140.
- "Their mouth is full of curses and bitterness" (v. 14). That's from Psalm 10.
- "There is no fear of God before their eyes" (v. 18). That's from Psalm 36.

But Paul is doing a strange thing that would have surprised

any devout believer familiar with those psalms. If you go back to those psalms, all those statements paint a stark us-versus-them picture. Those statements are prayed about and against the songwriter's enemies—people who are wicked, godless, completely bad. Some of those psalms, like Psalm 5, go so far as to create parallel contrasts, ping-ponging between what those wicked people do and what *I* do.

This is why Paul's argument comes as a shock. He uses these very psalms—these worship songs that tend to be sung to express and mourn moments that foster an us-versus-them mindset—and he shoves every last one of us into the "them" category. We thought "none is righteous" means "none of those people over there." And Paul increases the boundaries of inclusion: all are unrighteous. We're all in the same boat. We all need Jesus. "Us versus them" becomes "we."

This has some important implications for worshiping and worshipers. It means that not even sanctified Christians can claim any sort of high ground when they gather to exalt the name of Jesus and encounter the Holy Spirit. It means that in worship there are no special seats or privileged positions (James 2:1–4). It means that even the most well-behaved and godliest of Christians should approach God with as much fear and trembling as the uneasy, probably uncomfortable non-Christians who just might find themselves among us today.

It gives us an incredible compassion, patience, and humility before people who are different from us. And it levels the playing field of worship: we all come to the gathering with the same basic posture: needing Jesus.

Needing Jesus is *the* principal thing that Christians and non-Christians have in common. And if our worshipers wore that desperate dependence on their sleeves every week, I daresay we just might have the most attractive and beautiful worship culture out there. So let's join our hearts in prayer as we head into worship, asking God to elevate an atmosphere of dependence among us and obliterate any us-versus-them deception that could stifle that sweet air.

 **PRAYER**

Aim your prayers in this direction:

- Pray that God would destroy any feeling or thought of "us versus them" among your people today.
- Pray that the Holy Spirit would use the elements of the worship service to oppose the proud but give grace to the humble (Prov. 3:34; James 4:6; 1 Peter 5:5).
- Pray for non-Christians, that God would bring them to worship, that God would prepare the hearts and actions of your people to be hospitable, and that God would awaken their hearts to the good news of Jesus as he continues to do in our hearts.

# 18 | Our Sacrifice of Praise

**SCRIPTURE**

*Read Philippians 2:1–11.*

**DEVOTION**

It's a common story for people who give their time to facilitate worship services, whether they're the up-front people like the pastors and musicians, the in-back people, like the tech team, or the in-between people, like the ushers, greeters, and those who prepare communion or set up the room. There's a sacrifice made in being one of those people. It can sometimes be the case that as you're working through the details of logistics and leading others, a worshipful spirit is hard to find.

Chances are, part of the reason you serve is because you've had powerful experiences in worship. In the words of the writer to the Hebrews, you "have tasted the heavenly gift, and have shared in the Holy Spirit, and have tasted the goodness of the word of God" (Heb. 6:4–5). You've had those sweet moments in worship when God's presence felt so tangible, and you know what the psalmist means when he says, "It is good to be near God" (Ps. 73:28). You love worship and what God does there, and you started serving both because you wanted to be even nearer and because you wanted to help others "taste and see that the Lord is good" (Ps. 34:8).

But inevitably, something happens in the week-to-week, month-to-month grind of serving in and around worship services. The spirit of worship that was so easy to access seems elusive. And maybe you feel that the passionate fire that roared in your heart has dwindled to a handful of embers.

I've found three things to be true in these seasons of dryness when it seems that I'm serving a lot but not getting a lot. May they be words of comfort to you.

First and foremost, know that Jesus' love for you and the presence of the Holy Spirit do not depend on your ability to be in the right frame of mind or heart to receive them. It's a simple truth of the gospel that often evades us when we're struggling to find the joy of his presence. We can easily slip into the antigospel, anti-Christ idea that God's visitation depends on us—that somehow God won't meet us unless we're prayed up, cleaned up, and ready. Nothing could be farther from the truth that Paul declared when he said, "God shows his love for us in that while we were still sinners, Christ died for us" (Rom. 5:8). God visits because God loves us, not because we're ready. The truth is, we're never really ready. And that's a freeing word.

Second, know that God will surprise you in his faithfulness by visiting you with his presence even as you're serving, even as you're unprepared for him. I've had this happen to me, and maybe you have too. During dry seasons, when you least expect it, God will simply invade an otherwise dead moment. Sometimes it will be in the middle of a worship song or hymn. Sometimes it will be as someone else is praying or preaching. Sometimes it will be when the congregation's voice drowns out your own and you're swallowed up in the praise of heaven. But God has always been faithful in these unprepared-for, surprise visitations, and it's appropriate to ask for them and hope for them.

Third, know that leaders in worship are indeed called to offer a special sacrifice of praise. Though it doesn't feel worshipful, in God's estimation it is every bit as valid a form of worship. Philippians 2 tells us this. Just as Jesus emptied himself, so too can we know the joy of imitating his selflessness by looking not only to our own interests but also to the interests of others (Phil. 2:4), even in worship. It doesn't make us worship martyrs. It doesn't make us better than other people. And it certainly doesn't make God more pleased with us than he already is in Christ. But our sacrifice in caring about the details of worship so that others don't have to is an invitation to know the special joy of sharing in the self-emptying service of Jesus Christ. That we worry about the logistics so that our brothers and sisters are free is itself a sweet offering to the Lord, and it pleases the heart of the Father.

Take comfort that the words the Father eternally speaks over the Son are spoken over you: "This is my beloved . . . with whom I am well pleased" (Matt. 3:17).

 **PRAYER**

Aim your prayers in this direction:

- Pray that the Holy Spirit would make Jesus so beautiful and believable to you that the lie about our needing to be prepared and ready for his grace would vanish.
- Pray for those in your community who have experienced a long season of dryness, and ask the Lord to surprise them with a powerful sense of his presence, love, and grace.
- Pray for the Spirit to bear the fruit of joy in worship this week among all those who lead and volunteer in and around the worship services, that they would be empowered not only to offer their sacrifices of praise but also to enjoy them.

# 19 | The Face of God

*Read Psalm 114:1–8.*

### DEVOTION

I get a little squeamish when we sing hymns and worship songs that cry, "I want to see your face, Lord." The Old Testament repeatedly shows this to be a dangerous request. Whenever we see "face" and "presence" in Hebrew Scriptures, we can know that we're looking at the same Hebrew root word.

Nothing signals one's presence like one's face. We see this so clearly today in our bodily communication with one another and in our cries to be more present. My friends, my kids, my roommate, my spouse, or my family could be stationed in the same room as I am and not really be present to me. Why? Because their faces aren't before me. They are before their phones. Their faces are turned toward a device and away from my face. So we rightly understand: face unlocks presence.

Early on in God's dealings with humanity, he set the terms of engagement with regard to his face. Do you remember that famous encounter when Moses got a little bold? "Please show me your glory," Moses said, probably in desperation (Ex. 33:18). God's response shows the gravity of the request. "I'll do it," God said, "but . . . you cannot see my face, for man shall not see me and live" (v. 20). But unlike seeing the backs of people whose faces are buried in their screens, seeing God's glory is so powerful that even beholding his back gives us enough secondhand glow that we don't need to request any face time. To see God's back is presence enough for us—at least until he gives us new bodies that can withstand the full power of his face.

Psalm 114 gives us the right response to the face of God: "tremble" (v. 7). So if even Moses couldn't see God's face, why in the world would we ask for it? Well, it's because something has happened that has changed the terms of engagement forever. We've had an epiphany. A revealing.

John 1 tells us that in Jesus, we are able to see what Moses never could: the face of God. When the eternal Word became flesh, thenceforth humanity could cry with the beloved apostle, "We have seen his glory, glory as of the only Son from the Father, full of grace and truth.... No one has ever seen God ... [but Jesus] has made him known" (John 1:14, 18).

There's a name for Jesus that perfectly captures the paradox of face and presence in Scripture. We tend to sentimentalize it around Advent and Christmas, but this name can't be quickly domesticated, easily etched on an ornament, or casually scripted on a greeting card. Before Immanuel—"God with us"—was a name of comfort, it was a name of dread. If you read Isaiah 7 carefully, you see that Immanuel would come to judge God's people, to lay them to waste for their rebellion. "God with us" was not something to be desired without also preparing for judgment. And yet when Jesus came, the surprise to us all was that Immanuel came not to condemn the world but to save it (John 3:17). He came not to enslave but to be a ransom for many (Mark 10:45; Matt. 20:28). He came not to judge sinners but to be judged in the place of sinners (2 Cor. 5:21).

To desire "God with us"—to desire his presence and his face—apart from Jesus is a dreadful request and an impossible ask. But to seek God's face in Jesus—well, there's nothing better, nothing more desirable, nothing more satisfying. It's why Paul can say that all real transformation, in worship and in life, comes through beholding the glory (the presence) of Jesus "with unveiled face"

(2 Cor. 3:18). And it's why we can write and sing hymns and worship songs that mirror the audacious language of other psalms: "You have said, 'Seek my face.' My heart says to you, 'Your face, Lord, do I seek.' Hide not your face from me" (Ps. 27:8–9). "Seek the Lord and his strength; seek his presence continually!" (Ps. 105:4).

So by all means, when you gather for worship, seek, ask for, beg for the face of God. And then watch for Jesus to show up in the power of the Holy Spirit.

### ⤳ PRAYER

Aim your prayers in this direction:

- Ask the Holy Spirit to magnify the glory of Jesus Christ—who he is and what he has done.
- Pray that the Holy Spirit would prepare people's hearts to be open to encountering the face of the Lord—from being confronted by God's fearsome glory into the comfort of being known and loved through Jesus Christ.
- Pray for a spirit of anticipation in the hearts of all who gather for worship, that all would yearn for and seek the face of God in Jesus.

# 20 | Why Worship Isn't Always Fun

### SCRIPTURE

*Read Psalm 119:103.*

### DEVOTION

Many of us who grew up in the church remember those moments when some adult would teach us or spontaneously exclaim, "Worship is what heaven is going to be like!" And we kids would look at each other with covertly petrified glances, thinking the same thought in unison: "I sure hope not! Worship is boring. I don't get it. Everybody seems a tad uncomfortable, and if we're being honest, we're all thinking about lunch."

I'm afraid these early misgivings often carry themselves into adulthood. Perhaps we're a bit more mature, long-suffering, and willing to press through less than ideal circumstances because we're convinced (as we should be) that worship is worth it, but the fact is that many of us remain convinced: worship isn't fun.

And honestly, fun isn't the best word. To find something to be fun or not fun seems a bit flippant, a bit surfacy, for worship. So let's use a different word, a biblical word: satisfying. Think of the things to which we assign the word satisfying. That meal was satisfying. Why? Because it tasted good and it solved our hunger. That song was satisfying. Why? Because it sounded good and it took us to a place of rest or euphoria. That relationship is satisfying. Why? Because it seems to fill up a deficit within us, and it makes us feel like we're overflowing with love, lacking nothing.

When the psalmist gushes, "How sweet are your words to my taste, sweeter than honey to my mouth!" he is saying, "Your word is satisfying." For the psalmists, the Word of God does what a tasty meal does, a beautiful song does, or a deep relationship does.

And we need to remember that Psalm 119, long as it is, is still nothing more and nothing less than a worship song—lyrics and a melody intended to be sung by a group of people gathered for worship. Psalm 119 is one, big ode to the Scriptures. It's a worship song that sprints past infatuation into full-blown obsession with the Word of God. And verse 103 presses at least two thoughts on us:

First, because verse 103 is a worship-song lyric, we become aware that God's Scriptures should stand at the center of our gathered worship times. Not only Psalm 119 but the entire psalter is dedicated to singing the Word of God, giving us ample reason to believe that the worship service, as a whole, should be centered on and saturated with the Bible. Psalm 1, which most recognize as the psalter's great thesis statement, declares that a person is "blessed" when he or she meditates on God's Word day and night (Ps. 1:1–2). So our services, if they are to be satisfying, should be permeated with the Bible like a sopping sponge is permeated with water.

Second, though, verse 103 forces a question on us that has haunted some Christians since their childhoods: "Why don't I find worship satisfying like this?" Certainly we need to ask, "Well, just how Word-saturated is my worship service?" But there's another simple, biblical reason: sin. Sin is the great world flipper. The great twister. It takes what God created as straight and makes it, in the words of Habakkuk, "crooked" or "perverted" (Hab. 1:3–4). Sin takes something as straightforward as the satisfaction of Word-filled worship and distorts its simple pleasure into something else.

The Bible employs many words for sin, but one of the most frequent is what often gets translated as "iniquity." Iniquity is crookedness, bentness. And just like a tool that has been bent never quite works right, so we too are bent worshipers. And worship never comes out right, never feels totally right.

Psalm 119:103 presents a gap, then, between what worship should be and what worship often is. Worship should be satisfying, but it often leaves us wanting. It's often the kind of thing we hope heaven isn't like.

This gap can be hurdled only by the Holy Spirit. We need the Holy Spirit to take our feeble plans for worship, which are no doubt crooked, and make them straight. We need the Holy Spirit to take hearts, minds, bodies, and souls, which no doubt wrestle in the perversion of the flesh, and give them the kind of hunger and thirst that finds satisfaction only in God's Word and in his presence among his people.

This hunger isn't something we can conjure. Only the Lord can give it to us. And the satisfaction of a worship service that tastes sweeter than honey isn't something we can cook up ourselves. Only the Lord can be our host, our chef, our server, and yes, even our meal (John 6:53–56).

So are you hungry enough yet? Are you desperate enough yet? Well, guess what? Just as only the sick need a physician (Mark 2:17), so only the hungry will be truly satisfied by a meal of the Word of Christ. Your need, and the neediness of your church, is all that's required for entry. Come and worship.

### ⪜ PRAYER

Aim your prayers in this direction:

- Ask the Holy Spirit to lead you and your church toward a saturation in the Scriptures, both inside and outside the worship service.
- Pray desperately for the Holy Spirit to make the Word deeply satisfying to all who gather.
- Ask the Holy Spirit to close the gap between what worship should be and what worship often is, so that all might experience the sweetness and joy of Christ's presence.

- Pray for those who will take an up-front part in ministering the Word in the worship service—those who lead music, those who pray, those who preach, those who administer baptism and the Lord's Supper—that the Spirit would fill them and use them effectively.

# 21 | The Unbudding Fig Tree

*Read Habakkuk 3:17–19.*

 DEVOTION

It's a burdensome, tiring, and maybe unsustainable thing to worship God when you don't feel like it. Every human is wired for worship to have a holistic integrity. If I'm worshiping God, I should feel an alignment between the act of worship and how I feel about it. I should want to worship God.

Suffering has a way of sabotaging our "wanter." It's hard to rev up the motivation, the internal engine of worship, when difficulty and pain are overwhelming us. Bitterness sours everything, and joy feels like a real chore.

Thank God for the biblical songwriters who flooded the Psalter with worship songs that express the suffering and sing through it. And thank God for the musical prophet Habakkuk, whose short book not only prophesied a word to an Israel headed into exile but also modeled a faithful path for worshiping through suffering.

Habakkuk opens with a complaint against God, a complaint that's pretty defensible. He's received a word from the Lord about his people. He is to be the messenger of that word. He ponders that word and then recognizes rightly that something is not quite fair about God's ruling. And so Habakkuk opens with a "that's not fair, Dad!"

Habakkuk knows that Israel has rebelled against God and that Israel needs the Father's loving discipline. But he sees God's course of action as unjust. God has chosen to use the Babylonians—a far more pagan and wicked people—to mete out his justice on Israel. "It's one thing to punish us, God," Habakkuk says, "but it's another to do so by giving triumph to people who are far worse than we are" (Hab. 1:13).

And so Habakkuk folds his arms, closes his case, and basically says, "I'm going to wait to see what God has to say about *that*" (2:1). And as often happens when we make a lot of our seemingly airtight arguments against God, God puts Habakkuk in his place. God thunders back at Habakkuk, similar to the way God spoke to the sufferer Job when it was time. God reminds Habakkuk, "Remember who you're talking to, my child."

Humbled, Habakkuk yields, penning a prayer that sounds strikingly similar to the praise song in Psalm 18. The sufferer goes back to the old, familiar, well-worn worship songs that are baked into the memory of his heart. He goes back to simple faith and the simple act of being just a worshiper.

The act of pouring himself out in a worship song before the Lord leads to something—an addendum, a resolution at the close of the book, which we just read. This resolution states that "though the fig tree should not blossom, nor fruit be on the vines . . . yet I will rejoice in the LORD; I will take joy in the God of my salvation" (Hab. 3:17–18).

It's the counterintuitive discovery that to worship God through suffering—to worship God when we don't feel like it—has a mysterious way of strengthening our faith and aligning the desire to worship with the act of worship.

Every week, sufferers of all sorts limp into our worship spaces carrying seen and unseen burdens. Some sufferers are in such pain that the best they can do is sit in the back row and stare at the floor or quietly weep. There's a blessing in just being there. Sometimes sufferers are buoyed up when other Christians sing around them, sing *for* them. Other sufferers hide the pain by dressing up and going through the motions of singing, praying, receiving preaching, receiving grace at the table. There's a bless-ing there too. Sometimes God breaks through the numbness.

But with any kind of suffering, the book of Habakkuk stands as a testament that God is not distant from the sufferer in his or her moment of need. To the contrary, "The Lord is near to the bro-kenhearted and saves the crushed in spirit" (Ps. 34:18). So band together and take some time to pray for all the kinds of suffering that will be brought to the cross in the upcoming worship service, even and especially if it's your own.

 **PRAYER**

Aim your prayers in this direction:

- Pray for sufferers who may be struggling to decide whether to even come to church this week. Ask the Holy Spirit to bring them.
- Pray for sufferers who are knowingly or unknowingly bitter toward God. Pray that God's kindness and gentleness would be evident to them in worship.
- Pray for the tone of the worship service to be devoid of harshness and filled with the peace of God and the wooing love of the Holy Spirit.
- Pray that sufferers of all stripes would feel like worship is a safe enough space to lay that pain, honestly and authentically, before God and others.

# 22 | The Day of the Lord

### SCRIPTURE

*Read John 20:1–18 [for a shorter reading:
John 20:1, 6–7, 11–16].*

### DEVOTION

Worshiping on Sunday is a time-bending, mystical enterprise. Before Jesus' time on earth, believers in the one, true, living God worshiped on Saturday, the holy Sabbath. It was day seven of the week—the day of rest, joy, and delight, mirroring God's rest on the seventh day of creation (Gen. 2:1–3).

When Jesus rose from the dead on the first day of the week—Sunday—early Christians viewed this as such a cosmically significant event that they reoriented their worship practice. You think it's hard to change just one simple worship tradition in your church? Imagine changing a thousands-year-old tradition such as what day to gather for worship! Yes, Jesus' resurrection was that significant.

The gospel of John is full of parallels between the first book of the Bible, Genesis, and the story of Jesus. In fact, you could say that John is the Genesis of the New Testament. It begins just like Genesis does: "In the beginning." As John recounts the stories of Jesus in his gospel, he maps Jesus' life and ministry onto dozens and dozens of instances in the book of Genesis. He intends for the reader to think about God's creation of the world as he tells the story of the recreation of the world through Jesus.

It's purposeful, then, when John loads his resurrection account with a lot of Genesis-y allusions. Just like the earth was "without form and void" (Gen. 1:2), so the resurrection story begins "while it was still dark" (John 20:1). Adam and Eve's sin required shameful covering of their bodies (Gen. 3:7), but the New Adam, Jesus Christ, emerges from the grave uncovered, with "the linen cloths lying there," useless in the tomb (John 20:5). Adam and Eve walked in a garden (Gen. 3:8); a woman met Jesus alone, mistaking him for a gardener (John 20:15).

John's point is clear: through cross and resurrection, the old creation has died and the new creation has come. And this has some radical implications for worship.

Acts and Corinthians both report that Christians quickly began to gather for worship on Jesus' resurrection day, "the first day of the week" (Acts 20:7; 1 Cor. 16:2). In the book of Revelation, John the gospel writer reveals what Christians began to call this first day: they called it "the Lord's Day" (Rev. 1:10). This title isn't just some reference to how Sunday is Jesus' special day. No, "the Lord's Day" is another way of referring to a special Old Testament prophecy known as "the day of the Lord."

The prophet Joel speaks of the day of the Lord as the end of time and the final judgment when the sun would turn to darkness and the moon to blood (Joel 2:31). Amos describes the day of the Lord as a day of full and perfect justice for all who have been wronged (Amos 5:18–24). Just a few pages before the New Testament, the prophet Malachi describes the day of the Lord as an overwhelming refiner's fire, purifying everything (Mal. 3:3).

And crazy enough, Christians use this phrase—the day of the Lord—as the title of our worship day, Jesus' resurrection day.

Here's just one mindblowing implication of all this: when we gather for worship, God is bringing the future new heavens and new earth, promised in Revelation's final "day" (Revelation 21), into the present moment of worship. Imagine you're standing in a broad, low valley and ahead of you a mile or two is an enormous hundred-foot-high concrete wall, which is damming up a large body of water. On that wall is written "the day of the Lord."

When Jesus rose from the dead some two thousand years ago, it is as though he punched some holes into that wall, and now those future precious healing waters ahead of us are dribbling back to us at our feet whenever we gather for worship.

What was once wholly promised in the future has been unlocked and poured out in foretastes when we worship. You can almost taste those waters in the bread and wine of the table. You can nearly feel their cleansing as you witness a baptism. You hear them lapping up on the shores near your toes in preaching. You feel the bellows of their rhythmic waves in the music.

Worship is a time-bending, present experience of the future day of the Lord. It is the backward leak of the dammed up heavenly waters, meant to give us just enough hope and promise to help us make it through another week this side of eternity. When God calls us into worship, it is an invitation to experience all the peace, joy, and fullness of where we're headed.

 **PRAYER**

Aim your prayers in this direction:

- Pray that the Holy Spirit would fill your congregation with inspiring hope this Sunday.
- Pray for a powerful experience of the joy and peace of the future new heavens and new earth right in your midst as you worship.
- Ask, seek, and knock for God to graciously offer tangible foretastes of future healing of body and soul in your worship gathering.
- Ask God to tear down the cultural forces that would seek to make your church now-focused to the neglect of the future orientation and hope of the coming day of the Lord.

# 23 | Enter with Thanksgiving

 **SCRIPTURE**

*Read Psalm 95:1–2.*

 **DEVOTION**

We may breeze right by it. If we've been worshipers for any length of time, we've heard, read, or sung the phrase "enter his gates with thanksgiving" from Psalm 100:4. It's a staple call to worship which has been a part of historic Christian practice, embedded in some of our most ancient liturgies.

Entering with thanksgiving, whether we realize it or not, comes with at least one loaded assumption. It assumes that God has already been working, already been revealing, already been giving, already been speaking, even before we walked through the door. Even before God has acted and moved in our midst in public worship, he has been acting and moving "out there" in our lives, Monday through Saturday. And that means that we enter with something to thank God for.

This is why we can't buy into the lie of what some have called the sacred-secular distinction—the idea that certain times and places are devoted to the work of God, to religious practice and devotion, and then the rest of our life in the world is disconnected from that.

Gathered worship is never a retreat from the world. Gathered worship is the most worldly thing we do, in a sense, because it's the deepest expression of what it means to be human. Gathered worship reminds us, as we confess our sin and hear the Good News, that all of life is repentance. Gathered worship reminds us, as we partake of the Lord's Supper, that we live Monday through

Saturday sustained only by Jesus, the Living Bread (John 6:51). And gathered worship reminds us, as we come into his presence with thanksgiving, that all of life is a gift.

Two millennia ago, the apostle Paul asked the Corinthian church a potent rhetorical question: "What do you have that you did not receive?" (1 Cor. 4:7). He asks you and me the same question today. When we are instructed to enter God's gates with thanksgiving, Paul's challenging question hovers in the background. We could say it like this: "Monday through Saturday, haven't you seen that every good thing that came your way was a total gift from God? You have so much to be thankful for!"

This all means that we can't accept a disconnection between Sunday and the rest of the week. We are on the hook for being 24-7 worshipers. But this shouldn't be heard as a burden, as in, "You'd better be thankful and worship God Monday through Saturday." Rather, it should be heard as an invitation to open your eyes during the week to all the ways God is coming at you with gifts and graces. Because when our antennae are up to all the ways God is already working in our ordinary lives, we can't help but be thankful. We can't help but worship.

There is, therefore, a direct relationship between our Sunday gathered worship and our Monday-through-Saturday scattered worship. They feed off of each other and accelerate one another. If you're looking for new heat and vitality in a gathered worship time that's gone cold, try opening your eyes and ears to all the gifts you're receiving throughout the week. If you're looking for a more worshipful posture to your work week and day-to-day vocation, take the risk of pouring more of yourself out when God's people gather—more body, more emotions, and more passion.

And above all else, ask, seek, and knock (Matt. 7:7–11). Because even our thankfulness is ultimately a gift from God, it is a great practice to ask for it. So as we turn to God in prayer, let's ask him to send his Holy Spirit to fill us with gratitude.

 **PRAYER**

Aim your prayers in this direction:

- Pray for yourselves and your sisters and brothers who are gathering for worship, that all might be able to see just how much God has been faithfully working and graciously giving to them.
- Pray that believers in your church would find a deeper connection between the Sunday worship of the gathered church and the Monday-through-Saturday worship of their day-to-day lives.
- Pray for those who may be suffering acutely this week, who may have a harder time seeing the blessings and finding the gratitude. Pray that the Holy Spirit would supernaturally grant them thankfulness, even in this moment.

# 24 | Worship as Remembrance

 **SCRIPTURE**

*Read Psalm 66:5–7.*

 **DEVOTION**

The word *remembrance* is a really important Bible word, especially when it comes to worship. The Christian tradition, throughout the centuries, has zeroed in on this word as a key to unlocking an important facet of what we're doing when we're worshiping together. Worship in its deepest sense, they say, is remembrance.

Christians probably began fixating on this word because Jesus used it in connection with one of the most important rituals we engage in during worship—communion. In that famous passage from 1 Corinthians that many of us hear before we come to the table—what many traditions call "the words of institution"—Jesus says twice, "Do this in remembrance of me" (1 Cor. 11:24–25).

The basic meaning of *remembrance* is "recollection of something in the past." Remembrance is creating or reforming a picture of a memory, whether of a life-changing event, an impressionable moment, or what you had for dinner last night. But according to the Bible, those experiences are just the starting place for what remembrance really is.

To remember in the biblical sense isn't only to recall an event, it is to understand yourself as actually present there, powerfully united with the event's original participants. Remembrance, biblically, is the closest thing we have to time travel. Remembrance is to so identify with a past event that you are convinced that you were actually there.

Did you notice it in the passage we read? No, the word

remembrance isn't there. But the act of rich biblical remembrance is. In Psalm 66, we have a songwriter who lived generations past the time of Moses recalling the exodus and its famous moment—that great marker of redemption—the Israelites passing through the Red Sea. Listen carefully to the psalmist's language (and I'll help by emphasizing a few things):

> He turned the sea into dry land;
>> they passed through the river on foot.
> There did we rejoice in him.
>
> —PSALM 66:6

The psalmist understands what worship does. As the gathered assembly sings this worship song, the "they" of Israel's story becomes "us." The psalmist rightly understands that when it comes to the story of redemption, we were all there. You see, worship is a mystical time-travel. It thins the membrane between past and future.

When Jesus says that we partake of the bread and the cup in remembrance of him, therefore, we're not merely recalling his death on the cross. We are being transported there. We are so identifying with the event that we become one with it, once again. We are gazing up at our crucified Savior and finding ourselves there with him—or to use Paul's better language, *in* him. Through remembrance, Paul's words to the Philippians and Galatians become our words. I am "found in him, not having a righteousness of my own that comes from the law, but that which comes through faith in Christ" (Phil. 3:9), and I am "crucified with Christ. It is no longer I who live, but Christ who lives in me" (Gal. 2:20).

The famous Good Friday spiritual from the African American worship tradition asks, "Were you there when they crucified my Lord?" By remembrance, the faithful Christian always answers, "Yes."

There are many applications to explore about remembrance in worship, but let's focus on just one: We live in a cultural climate where personal identity has achieved nearly godlike status. Who I am, and who I feel myself to be on the inside, is increasingly unassailable. To challenge my understanding of my identity is tantamount to attacking my personhood and violating the core of who I am.

Remembrance challenges this by reminding Christians that their fundamental identity is *outside* themselves, *there* in Jesus. Now, of course, the Holy Spirit inhabits us in such a way that Christ himself *is* inside us (John 14:17; Rom. 8:9–11). But what we mean is that fundamentally who we are is found in Jesus and his work of redemption for us, not in ourselves and our work for God. And if worship is to take us *there*, it can only be by the power of the Spirit. And so we pray.

### ⤳ PRAYER

Aim your prayers in this direction:

- Pray for God's people to have a rich experience of biblical remembrance in worship.
- Pray for people to find space in worship to confess and let go of lesser identities to cling to Christ.
- Ask for the Holy Spirit's power, particularly so that the gospel of Christ's finished work would be so clear and powerful that people feel transported to, and present at, those saving events.

# 25 | The (Not So) Ordinary Work of the Holy Spirit

 **SCRIPTURE**

> *Read Romans 8:15–18.*

 **DEVOTION**

Where can we anticipate the working of the Holy Spirit in our worship services? We often look for ecstatic or euphoric moments as places where the Spirit moves—and they are. We often look for moments of power when the preacher's words seem to be on fire as places where the Spirit moves—and they are. But there are other places to be on the lookout for as well.

To explore this, we need to make an important observation that's often neglected: a worship service is one long prayer session. We sometimes speak of prayer as a part of the worship service, but that's really limiting the nature of prayer solely to those moments when heads are bowed and eyes are closed. Really, every part of a service is prayer. When we sing, we're talking to God. When we hear preaching, we're listening to God talking to us. When we give an offering, we are merely with our bodies acting out this prayer: "Jesus, take all of me." When we receive communion, we're hearing God say to us, "It's true. I love you."

When we recognize that worship is prayer, new fields of Scripture open before us. Passages about prayer become passages about worship too. Take, for instance, that most famous story about prayer when the disciples asked Jesus, "Lord, teach us to pray" (Luke 11:1). Given what we now know, we also recognize that Jesus would be teaching them—and us—how to worship. And then, Jesus gave us the Lord's Prayer.

We remember Jesus taught us to begin this prayer in a specific way. We begin by addressing God as "our Father." We realize even with the opening pronoun that we don't worship alone. We worship *with* one another because God isn't just my Father or your Father but *our* Father. But the epistle to the Romans tells us it's better than that.

Romans 8 teaches that it is by the Holy Spirit that we call to God the Father. This "Spirit of adoption . . . by whom we cry, 'Abba! Father!'" (Rom. 8:15) is therefore the enabler of the prayer we pray, the engine of the worship we bring. Worship, therefore, is a Trinitarian enterprise. When we approach "our Father," we are worshiping him *through* the Son, *by* the Spirit.

The encouragement to us today is that though we long for powerful, emotionally overwhelming encounters with the Holy Spirit, we shouldn't look past the ordinary ways the Spirit promises to meet us. The Spirit can be found every time we call God "Father," because it's only by the Spirit we can do so. So when you pray the Lord's Prayer in worship, or when you sing to God the Father in a worship song, you should recognize that in those moments, it's ultimately not you praying and worshiping as much as it is you being caught up in the Spirit's speaking, the Spirit's singing, the Spirit's work of worship.

This is especially good news to those of us who are going through a dry season, when God seems distant and out of reach. We have an opportunity here to take God at his Word, that even though we sometimes can't feel him, he is nevertheless there in all our "our Father"-ing. Perhaps then we can go to prayer in preparation for worship not only anticipating the surprising and overwhelming ways the Spirit might be among us but also asking God to open up all our senses to see, hear, feel, and know the Spirit's presence in the midst of our calling, addressing, and praying to God the Father.

**PRAYER**

Aim your prayers in this direction:

- Pray that God would open up your "spiritual senses" to recognize the presence of the Spirit as you worship and pray to "our Father."
- Pray especially for sisters and brothers who are going through a dry season in their faith. Ask the Spirit to offer a fresh visitation of his presence.
- End the prayer time by praying together the Lord's Prayer.

# 26 | Two More in the Battle

### ⤺ SCRIPTURE

*Read Romans 8:26–27, 33–34.*

### ⤺ DEVOTION

It's a trope in almost every movie that has an epic battle scene. We're talking about that moment when the hero has been knocked down and the rest of the forces of good have been defeated. All seems to be lost, and the viewer is left without hope. But then the reinforcements that we never thought would be there—nor even could be there—arrive. And even though it's a trope, we're moved by it, every single time.

I think of that now-classic battle scene at the end of *Avengers: End Game*, when Captain America stands alone before Thanos, exhausted and bloodied. Thanos's mighty army assembles, and Captain America in his "I could do this all day" courage, struggles to his feet and tightens the leather strap on his shield. We admire and pity him. He's headed to his death. But then, the sparking circles begin to appear—portals through which come the mighty reinforcements we all thought were gone for good. Seemingly every character from every last Marvel movie shows up, and with renewed boldness, Captain America growls, "Avengers, assemble!" And the war begins.

We should have a similar feeling every time we assemble for worship. It's not a metaphor to say that worship is war. God's inspired worship songs—the psalms—are filled with martial language. And Jesus' third and final temptation in the wilderness is evidence enough that, among all the things the enemy hopes to take down, distort, and supplant, he is opposed most of all to the worship of God (Matt. 4:8–10).

We're often tempted to think that we go to this battle alone, that we're left to ourselves. God has called us to worship, and we are obligated to assemble and give him glory. And though that's not entirely untrue, it falls painfully short of telling the story of God's involvement in worship. You see, every time we worship, God sends reinforcements. We're not alone. And these reinforcements aren't just ordinary beings. They're actually God himself. God comes alongside us to aid us in his own worship.

Christians talk a lot about the power of "prayer warriors" in our lives—people who are mighty in prayer, who go before God on our behalf. The Scriptures tell us that we have *the* two strongest prayer warriors surrounding us and leading the charge in the prayer battle of gathered worship: the second and third persons of the Trinity, God the Son and God the Holy Spirit.

Romans 8 tells us that the Son and Spirit are two advocates who are constantly interceding for us, two prayer warriors going ahead of us into battle. The Spirit goes ahead to pray the prayers that we don't know how to pray because either our minds and hearts are too small to pray rightly, or we're too beaten down by suffering to offer to God anything coherent (Rom. 8:26–27). The Son goes ahead of us to provide not only protection but also perfection. Our passage says that he is at the right hand of God interceding for us (v. 34), and we learn from the book of Hebrews that his advocacy is particularly the ongoing pleading of the perfection of his holy life (Heb. 7:23–28) and the finished work of his sacrificial death (Heb. 9:11–28).

What amazing news! As we come to worship, we are not alone in our quest for God and in our battle against the works of darkness. And not only do we have reinforcements, we also have the most powerful ones. Not only do we have advocates and defenders, we have the most convincing, most persuasive champions of grace and forgiveness—the Son and the Spirit, who both share in and enjoy the delight of God the Father. And they invite us, wherever we are—whether weary or energized, whether anxious or at peace—to join their ranks and fall in line behind their capable leadership. Fear not, O Christian, for the battle ultimately is not yours but God's (2 Chron. 20:15).

 **PRAYER**

Aim your prayers in this direction:

- Pray that worship today would be marked by a tangible awareness of the two advocates in your midst—the Son and the Spirit.
- Pray for sufferers in your congregation who particularly need a sense that the Spirit is with them, groaning their deeper, incoherent prayers. Ask for the peace and comfort that only the Spirit can give.
- Pray for those who feel guilty coming into worship—who are hiding secret sins and bearing shame too dark to utter. Pray that they would find the freedom of the Son's forgiving work so relieving and overwhelming that they are finally able to let go and worship in the light.
- Pray that those who greet people as they arrive, along with the other members of the worshiping body, would be used by God as "hands and feet" of the ministry of the Son and Spirit in the worship service, offering grace, compassion, and comfort to other worshipers.

# 27 | Glory

### SCRIPTURE

*Read John 17:1–5, 20–23.*

### DEVOTION

*Glory* is a worship word. In Greek, it reads *doxa*, from which we get our word *doxology*, which for us is a song of praise but literally means "a word of glory." If you wanted to develop a biblical understanding of worship from the ground up, a great place to start would simply be a word study of *doxa* from Genesis to Revelation.

One of the most potent glory passages in the Bible is John 17, what has been called Jesus' High Priestly Prayer. This prayer is important for many reasons. First, it shows us what lies at the center of Jesus' heart, because it's the last recorded lengthy prayer Jesus offers in the gospel of John before his crucifixion. Second, it gives us one of the best glimpses into the mysterious depth of intimacy between the persons of the Trinity. Jesus is talking tenderly to the Father in the power of the Holy Spirit.

And what do we find when we peer into Jesus' heart and into the mystery of Trinitarian love? Glory is all over the place.

Glory is hard to describe and define. It's almost better understood not by its definition but by its effects. The Hebrew word for glory is *kavod*, which carries the idea of heaviness or weightiness. The effect of glory is to press down on us, overwhelm us, envelop us.

In Jesus' prayer, we learn that glory is what makes the Trinitarian relationship tick. "Father, . . . glorify your Son that the Son may glorify you. . . . And now, Father, glorify me in your own presence with the glory that I had with you before the world

90

existed," Jesus prays (John 17:1, 5). From eternity past, the Trinity has been busy passing glory around. Father, Son, and Spirit constantly pour out glory to one another.

Then, Jesus surprises us. This amazing God-glory is something so beautiful, so joyful, so desirous, so overwhelming that our good God would never wish to keep it to himself. Jesus reveals his mission—why he came to earth and why he is headed to the cross. Jesus prays specifically for you and me, "that they may all be one, just as you, Father, are in me, and I in you, that they also may be in us. . . . The glory that you have given me I have given to them, that they may be one even as we are one" (vv. 21–22). The goal of salvation is to share the spoils of God's glory, to enjoy the rapture of union, of oneness, with God in Christ.

If sharing in the rapture of glory is the goal of salvation, it is certainly the goal of worship for you and me. When you read Jesus' prayer, you get the sense that it wasn't some ritual. It was an overwhelming experience, saturated with intimacy, depth, beauty, and power. Likewise, worship at its best can do the same thing. God's goal for worship, through Jesus and in the power of the Spirit, is to envelop us in his glorious presence. Yes, worship should be an *experience* of glory.

Twice in the prayer, Jesus says that he is the gateway to this glory. He claims boldly both at the beginning and the end of his prayer, "I have manifested your name to the people," and "I made known to them your name, and I will continue to make it known" (vv. 6, 26). This shows us clearly that if we want access to glory, we need to go through Jesus. Even more, Scripture testifies that Jesus is the gateway to God's glory because he *is* God's glory (Heb. 1:3). Do you want to experience glory? Look at Jesus. Our worship must therefore make much of Jesus and walk us through the story of his gospel. Christ-centered worship is Spirit-filled worship, which is glory-filled worship. If you want the glory, you need Jesus. So let's pray for just that as we ask the Lord to prepare our hearts for worship.

 **PRAYER**

Aim your prayers in this direction:

- Pray that the people of God would be overwhelmed by God's glory when you gather.
- Pray that the Holy Spirit makes Jesus more beautiful and believable to the hearts of all who come.
- Ask God to tear down the barriers and remove the distractions that often inhibit a rich experience of the glory of God.

# 28 | Worship as Confrontation

 **SCRIPTURE**

*Read Psalm 115:1–8.*

 **DEVOTION**

Worship is a place we go to have the sense knocked back into us. Why in the world would we need to sing a song like "not to us, O Lord, not to us, but to your name give glory" unless we actually entertained crazy thoughts like, "I should receive glory"?

Monday through Saturday knocks us around and fills our minds and hearts with all kinds of competing truth claims, distorted identities, and false promises. We begin to think lies are truth and the truth is a sham. Think, for instance, about how counterintuitive Jesus' teaching on the kingdom of God is. When he says things like you must receive the kingdom of God like little children (Matt. 11:25; 19:14) or the kingdom of God is like a mustard seed (Matt. 13:31–32), it is so shocking, so opposite of what we think of when we think of kingdoms. When we think of kingdoms, we think of forceful power. We think of military might. We think of conquest.

But think about it. Jesus' teaching on the kingdom of God shouldn't be surprising or counterintuitive. His kingdom is the creation God intended—the way it should have always been. That it *is* so shocking to us should tell us something both about our broken world and about the sin-distorted way we often process it. And this is where worship steps in. Weekly, gathered worship is, in a sense, an embassy of God's kingdom. It's heavenly soil on earthly territory. It's a place where the future is present for the experiencing.

Worship is like smelling salts, waking us up from our delusional swoon state, turning what we think of as our world upside down so we can see things the way God created us to see them—right side up.

Psalm 115:4–6 has us singing some right-side-up truth:

> Their idols are silver and gold,
>> the work of human hands.
> They have mouths, but do not speak;
>> eyes, but do not see.
> They have ears, but do not hear;
>> noses, but do not smell.

One of the jobs of worship is to confront our idolatry and call out the silliness of it all. In the ancient Near East, people were fully convinced that faces molded from silver and gold had special power to do godlike things for them. And so their idolatry needed to be put in its place: "It's just metal. And metal can't save you."

But we too come into worship having placed our trust in all kinds of things that can't save us. Perhaps we've poured our hope into our intelligence, thinking that our intellects will provide us with better jobs and more prestige. Perhaps we've poured our hope into our money, thinking that it can offer us lasting safety and security. Perhaps we've poured our hope into a key relationship that we either possess or wish we had, thinking that it can offer us the love and peace that have been so elusive.

And worship steps in to say, "It's all metal. It can't live up to the job description of Almighty God." You see, we come to worship to be arrested by a vision of God so glorious that it obliterates all the other vain pursuits and calls them out as idolatry.

This all sounds pretty harsh, doesn't it? Who wants to participate in something so brutal? But thankfully, when the idols have been torn down, the God we find on the other side is a tender, loving Father. He's not wagging his finger or saying, "I told you so." Instead, in Christ, he's extending his arms with a loud "I love you" and a warm "welcome home."

This journey—from idol obliteration to divine embrace—is the journey on which every weekly worship service should take us. It's the journey of repenting again, believing the gospel again, returning to God . . . again. This is a journey so complex and so deep that only the Spirit can lead us. We can't manufacture it or plan for it. We can only yield to it. And so we go to prayer, inviting, asking, begging the Spirit to do what only he can do.

 **PRAYER**

Aim your prayers in this direction:

- Pray that worship would feel like a safe space for people to let their guard down and be honest before the Lord and one another.
- Pray that God would graciously confront your idols, both individually and corporately, in gathered worship this week.
- Pray that God would send his mighty Holy Spirit to make Jesus more appealing and his kingdom more compelling than all the other lesser things onto which you hold.

# 29 | Christ Ascended

*Read Acts 1:6–11.*

 DEVOTION

The Christian worship tradition celebrates this event in Acts as "the ascension." We modern Christians often give Christ's ascension short shrift. We're big on his incarnation at Christmas. We also make a big deal about his death and resurrection. But what about Jesus' ascension? Is there important meaning bound up in that event, or was it just filler text or travel music so that Jesus could get from point A to point B?

Early Christians placed huge importance on the ascension for our everyday lives. When the early church began to annually celebrate significant events in the life of Christ, the ascension was one of the earliest days marked out for celebration. Our brothers and sisters who paved the way for us have something to say to us here and now.

First, the ascension reminds us that our worship can never be acceptable without a forerunner, without someone to bridge the gap between heaven and earth. Remember that the first Christians were Jews, and the idea of ascension was baked into their religious practice. In the Old Testament, ritual animal sacrifice was typically done in a series. Animals were killed as substitutes in a succession. After the sin offering, which symbolized purification, came what was called the burnt offering, which symbolized access. Another name for this second sacrifice was the "ascension offering," because all who offered it would watch its smoke rise from earth to heaven as a sweet aroma to the nostrils of the Father.

The ascension offering taught believers that we can't approach God on our own. We need a forerunner who goes before us with the clean hands and pure heart that we don't have. The book of Hebrews tells us that because Jesus did this, we have hope: "We have this as a sure and steadfast anchor of the soul, a hope that enters into the inner place behind the curtain, where Jesus has gone as a forerunner on our behalf" (Heb. 6:19–20). Because of the ascension, worshipers have hope!

Second, the ascension was necessary for us to receive the power and presence of the Holy Spirit. Jesus taught clearly, "If I do not go away, the Helper will not come to you" (John 16:7). Though his disciples couldn't fathom it, Jesus knew that there was something better in store for them—and us—than God-in-the-flesh walking beside us. Jesus knew that nothing is better than God the Spirit *inside* us. Pentecost couldn't happen without the ascension. Likewise, worship full of the power and presence of the Holy Spirit in our midst requires Christ's rising to the right hand of the Father. You can't have one without the other.

Third, the ascension means that you and I have the strongest advocacy imaginable. You and I, even while straining to believe in Jesus, struggle with sin daily, hourly. We cave in; we succumb. We put ourselves too often before others, and we often leave good things undone which we should have done. Though Jesus' sacrifice was a once-and-for-all, "it is finished" sacrifice (Heb. 10:11–14; John 19:30), you and I need the psychological and spiritual comfort of knowing that the once-and-for-all work is always before the heart and mind of God the Father. We need ongoing advocacy for Christ's finished work.

Imagine you committed a serious crime and were up for trial. It's one thing to hire a seasoned, talented, successful defense attorney. It's quite another when that successful attorney is your own flesh-and-blood brother. Think about the intimate love and advocacy, compassion, and empathy beating out of the chest of

Jesus Christ our advocate, who, because of his intercession, guarantees our place before the Father and our adoption as daughters and sons into the Trinitarian family of glorious joy!

"Consequently, he is able to save to the uttermost those who draw near to God through him, since he always lives to make intercession for them" (Heb. 7:25). Yes, Jesus' ascension means everything for worship.

### ⤳ PRAYER

Aim your prayers in this direction:

- Offer prayers of gratitude and thanksgiving that Jesus has ascended and gone before us to plead the merit of his blood and to ongoingly offer prayers on our behalf.
- Pray specifically for people who are feeling vulnerable, guilty, shameful, or unworthy. Pray that the Holy Spirit would woo them with the love of their ascended advocate, Jesus Christ, and would offer the comfort of the gospel to them in the worship service.
- Pray that the overwhelming feeling and impression of today's worship service would be one of comfort and support, and that believers would mirror that gentleness and grace in the way they interact.

# 30 | Jesus Time

### SCRIPTURE

*Read John 6:41–51.*

### DEVOTION

Many wonderful devotions, teachings, and sermons have been dedicated to unpacking what are called the "'I Am' statements" of the gospel of John. Throughout the first half of that gospel, Jesus makes these shocking claims: "I am the bread" (6:35, 41, 48, 51); "I am the light of the world" (8:12); "before Abraham was, I am" (8:58); "I am the door" (10:7, 9); "I am the good shepherd" (10:11, 14); "I am the resurrection and the life" (11:25); "I am the way" (14:6); and "I am the vine" (15:1, 5).

The reason these statements are shocking and provocative is because Jesus is claiming the most sacred name of God, "I Am," for himself. This name, often translated into English as "Yahweh" or in older English Bibles as "Jehovah," is signaled every time our Bible translations capitalize the name "Lord." It's the special name God gave when Moses basically said, "You're the God who is about to redeem us, so what do you want us to call you?" God responded, "Call me, 'I Am'" (Ex. 3:13–14). And Jesus clearly was saying, "That same God—yes, that's me." In Jewish culture (unless you really are God, of course), that's heresy and blasphemy.

Still, one of the ideas less often observed about many of Jesus' "I Am" statements in the gospel of John is their significance in the context of Jewish worship and how that significance applies to Christian worship. Especially in chapters five through ten, Jesus' "I Am" statements coincide with certain Jewish feasts and festivals clearly signaled by John.

For instance, when Jesus says, "I am the bread of life" (6:35), we need to rewind to the beginning of the same chapter to understand the context in which he's saying it. John 6:4 says, "the Passover, the feast of the Jews, was at hand." Not only, then, is Jesus connecting himself to the manna in the wilderness (6:31) and, in claiming to be the bread, is he making a statement about his divinity, but also he's claiming to be the center of their worship practice. "Do you see that Passover bread—that symbol of God's redemption of your ancestors from slavery? Yes, that bread is about *me*," he claims.

Even less obvious to us is the significance of Christ's claim, "I am the light of the world" (8:12). We know from a chapter earlier that Jesus made this claim when "the Jews' Feast of Booths was at hand" (7:2). Though we wouldn't know this, a first-century Jew would: one of the important rituals enacted during the Feast of Booths was a lighting ceremony every evening, where four huge lamps were lit. But on the last night of the feast, the main lamp would remain unlit, symbolizing that Israel still awaited salvation to come. And onto this scene steps Jesus, claiming to be the light of the world.

We could look at a few more instances where Jesus continues to point to Israel's annual feasts and festivals to make the bold claim, "That's about me!" But the point is coming into focus. God's design is that our sense of time should revolve around the person and work of Jesus Christ. No wonder ancient Christians felt compelled to develop an annual worship calendar that moved from anticipation, to his nativity, to his childhood, to his ministry, to his death, to his resurrection, to his ascension, and to his sending of the Holy Spirit!

If we're honest, we don't typically feel time this way. We feel time much more according to the rhythms of the school year—with summer breaks and fall kickoffs. Our annual rhythms may still echo, like faded fifth-generation photocopies, some semblance of Jesus' rhythms. In a certain sense, Christmas is still a big deal culturally in many places. But by and large, we tend to feel time being punctuated far more by the Hallmark calendar or the anchor holidays of our nation than we do by the rhythms of the life of Christ.

In the gospel of John, Jesus challenges this. He says, "I don't just want your daily time, I want your yearly time." Everything is about Jesus. Or as the Scriptures say, "For from him and through him and to him are all things" (Rom. 11:36). Still, this doesn't have to put a burden on Christians that we all *have* to engage the church calendar year. Some of us may come from traditions that have some understandable concern about that. What this presses us to reckon with, though, is that worship should be a place that, among other things, recenters our sense of time on Jesus, overwhelming us with his sovereignty and lordship. It offers us an invitation to enjoy another facet of our "in Christness." Even as the earth takes another spin around the sun, we can enjoy the comfort and security of our own centered revolutions around God the Son.

##  PRAYER

Aim your prayers in this direction:

- Because people come to worship with many burdens related to time ("How am I going to get it all done?" "How much longer do I have here?"), pray that the Holy Spirit would help believers put those concerns and burdens into perspective today.
- Pray a bold, long-term prayer that God would shape the hearts and minds of the people in your church more according to Jesus' life and work and less according to any competing rhythms of culture.
- Pray that the person and work of Jesus would so overwhelm the gathered worship service today that time's center would be reestablished and provide an anchor strong enough to hold your flock until the next time you gather.

# 31 | The Spillover

## SCRIPTURE

*Read Psalm 139:1–18.*

## DEVOTION

I once heard a preacher say, "Worship begins when knowledge of God spills over from head to heart." That has always stuck with me, and I find it to be not only simple and profound but also biblical. The author of the worship song Psalm 139 expresses this spillover when he exclaims, "How precious to me are your thoughts, O God! How vast is the sum of them! If I would count them, they are more than the sand" (vv. 17–18).

On the experience side, I've had many Sundays when worship just stayed up there in my head. There was no spillover, no moment when it seemed like the entirety of me kicked in. Some people are leery of spillover. "Emotions are dangerous; they can lead you astray," they say. And while there is some truth to grapple with there, I've found it more dangerous, after nearly four decades of being a worshiper, *not* to have my emotions engaged. There's something incomplete, something subhuman about robotically engaging worship only in your head. And I know this from experience.

The Scriptures corroborate this. The Great Commandment urges us to love God with everything—heart, soul, mind, and strength (Deut. 6:5; Matt. 22:37). Emotions and feelings have to be included in the everything, no doubt. The psalms teach us this too. They use evocative, emotional language to describe the way we should talk to God. They model what worshipfulness should look like. And yes, worshipfulness looks like that overwhelming spillover when knowledge of God moves from head to heart, when contemplation breaks out into wonder, when seeing turns into beholding.

How do we find and cultivate that worshipful spirit? Comparing seeing to beholding is a good way to get at that elusive whole-self engagement. I remember a time when I beheld my wife, Abby. It was on our wedding day. Of course, I had seen her many times before. I could have reported to you a bunch of knowledge about her I had from seeing her. Abby has blue eyes and blonde hair, she doesn't like surprises, and she's always looking for the fastest, most efficient way to get from point A to point B. But reporting all of these observations stays in the realm of seeing. Things were very different on our wedding day.

When I saw her walking down that aisle, my knowledge of her spilled over from head to heart. I couldn't help it. I was overwhelmed. She reminded me of Jesus' love for the church and the way he makes her spotless. Seeing her gave me an overwhelming picture of our entire hopeful life together—the kids we didn't yet have, the stages of life, the grief and the joy, and the growing old together. All those things and more were bottled up in this one moment when I *beheld* Abby.

There is a similar dynamic at play for the worshiper who yields her or his imagination to the overwhelming wonder of who God is and what he has done. It's one thing to assent to the fact that "Jesus died on the cross for my sins." It's quite another to, in the words of hymn-writer Isaac Watts, "survey the wondrous cross," where "sorrow and love flow mingled down."

Beholding certainly includes practical things like letting our guard down and letting ourselves feel. It also includes saying no to the ten-thousand distractions—whether it's a squealy sound system, a phone buzzing in your pocket, a screaming baby, or an off-key song leader or out-of-tune instrument. Beholding often takes preparation and prayer, like what we're doing right now: quieting our spirits to be centered, listening, waiting, and available. Beholding involves expectation, like the psalmist who is so eager to worship that he impatiently cries out, "I will awake the dawn!" (Ps. 108:2).

But before we start feeling too guilty that the spillover of worshipfulness tends to show up a minority of the time, we should also recognize that it's human to go through dry seasons. Sometimes, they're so long that we've forgotten the joy of beholding, and we need David's faithful prayer, "Restore to me the joy of your salvation" (Ps. 51:12). The spillover of worshipful beholding is something God desires for us. Why wouldn't he want us to be overwhelmed by him? What wouldn't be good, right, true, and wholesome about that? Ultimately, the spillover can't be manufactured. It only can be given and received. So let's turn now to the Giver and ask for it.

 **PRAYER**

Aim your prayers in this direction:

- Pray against all the barriers and distractions that create divided attention and allegiance in worship.
- Pray—even beg—for the Holy Spirit to overwhelm your worshiping body with a wondrous sense of beholding the goodness, glory, and salvation of God through Jesus Christ.
- Pray for those sisters and brothers who have been in extended seasons of dryness. Ask the Holy Spirit to gently, but powerfully, meet them in gathered worship today.

# 32 | Always Repenting

### SCRIPTURE

*Read Psalm 107:1–16, 39–43.*

### DEVOTION

Psalm 107 is a longer psalm. We just read the opening and closing sections, but we missed about half of it. We wanted to read enough of it, though, that we got its flavor and pattern. It's a repeating psalm. After its preamble, it walks through four cycles, where it does the same thing over and over again. Here's the pattern of those cycles:

- People were broken, sinful, and helpless.
- Then they cried to the Lord in their trouble, and he delivered them.
- Let them thank the Lord for his steadfast love.

Four times it does this. Like a good, long, modern worship song, it has verses, a repeated chorus, and even a repeated second chorus. Each cycle has a slightly different theme, but they all share a pattern. Cycle 1 deals with the turmoil of anxiety and the resulting sense of starvation and desperation that flows from that (vv. 4–9). Cycle 2 deals with physical and spiritual slavery, which takes many forms today, including addiction (vv. 10–16). Cycle 3 deals with the crookedness of sin—what the Bible calls "iniquity"—and the way it tends to bend and distort our desires and moral compasses (vv. 17–22). And Cycle 4 deals with suffering and loss, the kind of pain that happens when an afflicted world happens upon you (vv. 23–32).

In each cycle, there's always the same response of the people: "Then they cried to the LORD." And God likewise has a same response: "He delivered them." And in response to that, there's yet something else that the people do: they thank the Lord for his steadfast love. At the end of the psalm is a loaded final statement. It feels even a bit ominous, like it should be heard with some echoing reverb: "Whoever is wise, let him attend to these things; let them consider the steadfast love of the LORD" (v. 43).

Though at first blush it sounds like a warning, you realize it's actually a blessed invitation: "Hey, if you're smart about this—about these cycles we just walked through—you'll stay there. Because if you stay there, well, that's where you'll find God's love."

What's the point of this psalm? We could sum it up in one statement: we never graduate from repentance. And that is a good thing.

In some Christian circles, sixteenth-century-reformer Martin Luther gets some fresh airtime every October because some five centuries ago in that month, the watershed moment that signaled the Reformation happened: Luther nailed his ninety-five theses to the door of the church in Wittenberg, Germany. Many Christians know of the event. But I wonder whether many Christians have read the ninety-five theses. You don't need to get very far in reading them to hear something profound. In fact, the first thesis is worth the price of the whole thing.

The first statement of the ninety-five theses boils the Reformation rediscovery of the gospel down to its essence. It says this: "When our Lord and Master Jesus Christ said, 'Repent' (Matt. 4:17), he willed the entire life of believers to be one of repentance."

What Luther meant by that, and what the cycles of Psalm 107 teach us, is that we never graduate from repentance. The great "work" of the Christian is always twofold: first, to confess our sin and need to God; and second, to cling to Jesus for everything. That, in a nutshell, is what repentance is.

Though Psalm 107 is a biblical worship song, it also teaches us an unassailable pattern for worship. A worship service, if nothing else, is simply a group of broken people walking through repentance together. Because the Christian life, in its essence, is daily repentance, so gathered worship, in its essence, is weekly repentance. Worship at its best is a distilled version of what our whole lives should be. And Jesus willed that our whole lives should be repentance.

And yes, this may be a challenge in two ways. For some of us, it may challenge the structure of our worship services. Perhaps we need to consider how to conform our services more to a structure of repentance—of confession, lament, and forgiveness. For others of us, it challenges the structure of our hearts. What is it that we really come to worship for? Do we come for a quick fix or an uplift? If it's not deep, death-and-resurrection-style repentance, then there's something to check. And there's certainly something to pray for.

 **PRAYER**

Aim your prayers in this direction:

- Pray for those who design, administer, plan, and lead worship services in your church. Pray that even their preparation might be marked by repentance.
- Ask the Holy Spirit in the upcoming service to lead people powerfully through the process of repentance.
- Pray for every worshiper—that their hearts would be soft, ready, and eager to pour out everything before the Lord.

# 33 | Lamentation as Praise

**SCRIPTURE**

*Read Psalm 149.*

**DEVOTION**

Over the last few decades in much of the Western church, we've seen a fresh awakening to and embracing of the ancient, biblical practice of lamentation. Lament has always been a prominent posture of prayer in the Scriptures. It is even one of the Bible's earliest themes, if we believe with many that the book of Job is the earliest written book in the Bible. (The first five books cover the earliest events in human history but were recorded by Moses and were therefore authored later than Job.)

Many have noted that the church has absorbed too much of modern Western culture's allergy to pain and suffering, resulting in the muscles of lamentation largely becoming atrophied. Perhaps, in catering to consumer mindsets, we've opted for "happy church" because we think a therapeutic positivity is what people want. Perhaps, in caving to the culture's pursuit of a forever-youthful and pain-free life we've lost the rich, biblical tradition of praying our pain out loud to God in holy, hopeful complaint.

But it seems that as culture has become more fractured, and as answers to problems seem more complex than ever, lamentation has reemerged in the life of the church like treasure buried right under our pews. So many churches are engaging our tradition of lamentation afresh!

Many of the best worship thinkers have reminded us in the middle of this rediscovery that much of the global church and even sectors of Western Christianity never lost the practice of lamentation. Often, many of us overlook these pockets of health because they tend to exist on the margins of our majority cultures.

For instance, I've been reminded by my believing African American friends that the black church has always been lamenting in worship, and its tradition just might be one of the richest storehouses from which to freshly draw insight, wisdom, and faithfulness in this aspect of worship.

Not long ago, some of my African American sisters and brothers reminded me of a "style" of lamentation that I'm hearing less about in my circles but certainly fills the Scriptures and saturates the black worship tradition. We could call it lamentation as praise. Psalm 149 is a classic example of this kind of lamentation.

Lamentation as praise fights against our intuition that one can *either* lament or praise. It fights against our intuition that though some lamentation should look sad, morose, sorrowful, or angry, not all lamentation should. Lamentation as praise means that one form of crying out to God against injustice looks like stubborn joy and willful revelry, almost like acting as though the world is a better place than it really is because one day, in Christ, it will be.

Psalm 149 starts just like any other classic praise psalm would: "Praise the LORD! Sing to the LORD a new song. . . . Let them praise his name with dancing" (Ps. 149:1, 3). But then it takes a turn that only people from lamentation-as-praise traditions understand. Verses 6 and 7 get downright violent as they sing, "Let the high praises of God be in their throats and two-edged swords in their hands, to execute vengeance on the nations and punishments on the peoples."

People who don't know lamentation as praise cock their heads at this. But people who know what it's like to praise God when everything is hitting the fan understand exactly what this kind of worship is all about. In lamentation as praise, joy is a choice as much as it is an emotion. Praise is a decision as much as it is a feeling. Lamentation as praise is the "leather" of worship styles:

it's made tough and mature through being well weathered. And it comes only through practice.

Lamentation as praise sometimes gets confused with its illegitimate cousin, head-in-the-sand praise. Sometimes those who are in lamentation-as-praise mode look like they're ignoring their problems and pretending that everything is okay. They look like they're naively escaping their troubles. But that's only a superficial read on the situation, and often it is oblivious to the category of Psalm 149–style worship.

Perhaps your church community is ready to try this kind of lamentation. If so, you just might have to write your own songs. Or you might have to offer up spoken prayers of lamentation around or in the middle of songs that are more "pure praise." This is an underserved genre in current worship practice. Like any other form of worship, it takes practice, trust, commitment, and risk. But the payoff is worth it. Whether it's this week or some future week, perhaps it's time to begin praying that God would increase this practice in the hearts of your people, where joy and sorrow go hand in hand, and where "Praise the Lord!" really does become a battle cry.

 **PRAYER**

Aim your prayers in this direction:

- Pray that God would grow your congregation's ability to publicly lament in worship.
- Pray that God would increase your congregation's categories of lamentation to include praise.
- Pray that the Holy Spirit would break open hearts, minds, and bodies for fresh outpourings of authenticity and sacrificial worship in your community.

# 34 | The Goal of Redemption

### SCRIPTURE

*Read Exodus 3:11–12.*

### DEVOTION

What is the purpose of redemption? What is the endgame of salvation? Where is God's work within us driving us, taking us to? Many answers from the Bible are satisfying. We could say, with some accuracy, "We are saved so that we can be with God in heaven." We could say, with some accuracy, "We are saved so that we can love our neighbors."

We shouldn't overlook, though, one of the Bible's pervasive answers to the question of redemption's purpose: worship. Again and again, the entire Bible looks back upon the exodus of Israel as the prevailing metaphor for what Jesus came to do. Just as Moses came to lead Israel out of Egyptian slavery through the Red Sea, so Jesus leads us out of our spiritual bondage (Rom. 8:15; Gal. 4:4–7) through the baptismal waters of his death and resurrection (Rom. 6:3–4; 1 Cor. 10:1–4).

Given how significant the exodus is to the Christian story, we shouldn't overlook the theme that not only begins the exodus story but punctuates it throughout. The passage we just read is situated in Moses' famous burning-bush call from God. And God makes clear the purpose of his redemption: "When you have brought the people out of Egypt [redemption], you shall serve God on this mountain [worship]" (Ex. 3:12). If you think that interpretation is a stretch, just remember that the root word for *serve* in the Old Testament has to do with the kind of service one offers in corporate worship.

After our passage here in Exodus 3, God makes this point no less than thirteen more times in this and the next seven chapters (3:18; 5:1, 3, 8; 7:16; 8:1, 20, 25–29; 9:1, 13; 10:3, 7–11, 24–27). God is serious about getting the message across: the goal of redemption is worship. This teaches us at least three things:

*First, God thinks gathered worship is really important.* In English, we have one word, *worship*, that houses a multiplicity of meanings. With that word we could mean the whole-life orientation of the self. We could also mean the activity of churches when they gather weekly. As we said, the Bible's language in Exodus 3—the word translated "serve"—specifically refers to the rituals and actions of the public worship of the people of God: praying, singing, sacrificing, preaching. God is redeeming Israel so that Israel can be freed to do those things. Likewise, he redeems us so that we can freely participate in public worship. We should take the epistle to the Hebrews seriously when it encourages us not to forsake meeting together for worship (Heb. 10:25).

*Second, the goal of evangelism is worship.* We don't evangelize people simply to make converts. We tell people about Jesus so that God can make worshipers out of them. We could say that when we share the gospel with others, we are participating in God's great "factory recall" of all the broken and mis-aimed worship out there. God's intention for salvation is to refurbish (or to use a most biblical word, resurrect) his creation (2 Cor. 5:17) to recover creation's original purpose and design: worship.

*Third, worship is one of the most important fundamentally human things we do.* If we are being refurbished to worship God—if redemption's activity is to restore us to our original capacity and design—we learn from this that to be restored as a worshiper is to regain our lost humanity and deepest identity. Humanity's search for the meaning of life has always had its best answer in the worship of God. What am I doing here? What are you doing here? We exist to worship. The more we worship and exercise those forgotten muscles, the more we recognize it as a good, wholesome, and natural activity. We will eventually say, "I was made to do this, and it feels good!"

As we prepare for worship, let us go into it with all the joy, fervor, and expectation bound up in this rich theology of worship. Encourage each other, all the more, that what we're doing is not only worthwhile but also the best thing we could be doing. Strain to lift each other up to this high calling of corporate worship and enjoy the deep satisfaction of fulfilling one of your basic purposes.

## PRAYER

Aim your prayers in this direction:

- Pray that the Holy Spirit would enliven worship to be something more than dead ritual or meaningless practice. Ask for fresh movements of the living and active Word among you.
- Pray for people struggling to find meaning in worship, who for various reasons are stuck in a season of dryness or going through the motions. Intercede on their behalf.
- Pray for people struggling to find meaning in life. Pray for those who are depressed or who feel aimless or purposeless. Ask God to reveal himself in a tangible way that allows these individuals to find deeper meaning for their lives in and through worship.

# 35 | More Than We Can See

**SCRIPTURE**

*Read Revelation 7:9–12.*

**DEVOTION**

Do you ever look out on the gathered worshiping body of people and get discouraged? Something has drawn you into the ministry of worship. Some passion has prompted you to serve and kept you coming. And then maybe you look out at God's people and don't always see that same passion there.

Sometimes the discouragement is because some people seem so lifeless, disconnected, and disinterested. "We're in the presence of Almighty God, here!" we think. "How could you possibly yawn or check your phone?" Other times the discouragement is because not everyone is present and the room feels empty or underpopulated.

In those moments, it's important to seize the vision of worship given us by Revelation 7. This passage challenges us to close our physical eyes and strain our spiritual eyes to see what can be witnessed only by faith.

Revelation is one of those books that punches a hole in the wall between earth and heaven. And through that hole, we witness "a great multitude that no one could number, from every nation, from all tribes and peoples and languages, standing before the throne and before the Lamb, clothed in white robes, with palm branches in their hands, and crying out with a loud voice, 'Salvation belongs to our God who sits on the throne, and to the Lamb!'" (Rev. 7:9–10).

What we are witnessing is not just *a* megachurch. We are witnessing *the* megachurch that puts all our earthly megachurches to shame. Our megachurches, relatively speaking, are quite small and homogeneous. The heavenly megachurch makes our stadiums look like shacks and our multiethnic metropolises look like ingrown ghettos. And right now, the beautiful, heavenly megachurch is all gathered around Jesus, ceaselessly praising his salvation story, heaping loud, explosive, eternal glory onto the Lamb who was slain before the foundation of the world.

We could say that the worship of the heavenly church is a long, ever-flowing stream of worship. And here's the mindblowing part: when we gather for worship in our spaces—whether it's a theater, an old church building, a warehouse, a storefront, a field, or a living room—when we cross the threshold into those spaces, we step into that already moving stream and we join the song already being sung.

That means that when we gather for worship, we are always participating in something that is more than meets the eye. Our eyes often betray us, and we get discouraged. We see the sparse attendance or the lackluster participation and we wonder, "Is this all there is?" But the eyes of faith see the truer story.

You see, you just think you've come to *your* church. "But," the writer to the Hebrews says, "you have come to Mount Zion and to the city of the living God, the heavenly Jerusalem, and to innumerable angels in festal gathering, and to the assembly of the firstborn who are enrolled in heaven, and to God, the judge of all, and to the spirits of the righteous made perfect, and to Jesus, the mediator of a new covenant, and to the sprinkled blood that speaks a better word than the blood of Abel" (Heb. 12:22–24).

When we gather for worship, those you know who have died in the Lord—family, friends, loved ones—they're all there too. When we gather for worship, Christians from centuries past are all there too. When we gather for worship, God's armies of angels are there too. And most important, when we gather for worship, Jesus is there! May the Holy Spirit give us the eyes of faith to see these truer realities.

**PRAYER**

Aim your prayers in this direction:

- Pray that the Holy Spirit would impress upon the hearts and minds of all gathered for worship that they are part of a community much bigger than they can see.
- Pray for fresh wind from the Holy Spirit to energize the worship of those who are gathered to pray and praise with hopeful abandon.
- Ask the Holy Spirit to eliminate the distractions and discouragement that often take away from gathered worship that is wholly given over to the Lord.

# 36 | God-Fearing

**SCRIPTURE**

*Read Psalm 34:8–14.*

**DEVOTION**

In the Bible, there is no single word for worship. When you see the word *worship* in English, several different Hebrew or Greek words could be behind what you are reading. And some of those words don't always get translated into English as "worship."

Even this knowledge should tell us something about worship's complex and wide-ranging nature. One of the Hebrew and Greek worship words has perhaps more expansive reach than any other in the biblical vocabulary. That word often gets appropriately translated as "fear" in English. It's present in our passage: "Fear the Lord, you his saints, for those who fear him have no lack!" (Ps. 34:9).

*Fear*, as a worship word, is so central to our faith that it appears across Scripture as a title describing what we as the people of God are called. We are labeled "God-fearers" (Ps. 22:23; Acts 10:22). This worship word presses against any idea that worship can be contained in an hour or two on a Sunday morning. Do a word search on *fear* and you're thrust onto a playing field that stretches over all of life. *Fear* covers attitude and disposition. It covers behavior and action. *Fear* means that worship isn't merely the ritual of our gathered experiences. It's a lifestyle.

Fear as worshiping God means that we take Jesus seriously when he says that the greatest commandment is to love God with everything—heart, soul, mind, and strength (Matt. 22:37–38). Our passage here in Psalm 34 fleshes this out for us. "Come, O children, listen to me; I will teach you the fear of the LORD" (Ps. 34:11). And what does this God-fearing, worshipful lifestyle look like? "Keep your tongue from evil and your lips from speaking deceit. Turn away from evil and do good; seek peace and pursue it" (vv. 13–14).

All of life, Monday through Saturday, is our sanctuary. Our worship of God includes our wallets, our relationships with our classmates or coworkers, our political engagement, our retirement accounts, and our leisure time. My phone is a house of worship, where I am to fear the Lord. My email inbox and online shopping cart are holy tabernacles where I pour myself out in God's presence. When the psalmist says that he will "teach you the fear of the LORD," he is saying, "Come, let me teach you how to worship God 24-7."

This God-fearing, integrated worship life has a couple of implications: First, we need to fight the urge to be two different kinds of people when we're "at church" and when we're "in the world." To be a God-fearer means that we know no such distinction. We recognize that when we leave the worship space, we don't stop worshiping. Rather, we carry it forth into the world. We take the sweet-smelling fear of the Lord, replenished and bottled up on Sunday, and we pour it out like an alabaster jar of perfume on Jesus' feet Monday through Saturday. We recognize the holy moments embedded in the ordinary rhythms of eating, conversing, phone scrolling, and Netflix watching.

Second, we can let gathered worship establish patterns for how we worship scattered out in the world. Part of what a good worship service does is boil life down to its essential elements. It reminds us what being human is fundamentally about. It grounds our identity as God's creatures, made in his image, redeemed by his Son, filled with his Spirit, and then restored to receive and give love.

Worship also teaches us one of our most important skills. We could even call it *the* pro hack for being the best human this side of eternity. The Bible and the Christian tradition call this skill repentance—the art of being so secure in Jesus' love that we're free to own, out loud, our sin and baggage in front of other people, to apologize, and to seek forgiveness and restoration from God and others. If we learn nothing else from worship but how to be good penitents (repenters), we have been equipped with the most important skill for being a 24-7 God-fearer.

The integrated, God-fearing life doesn't come easy. Everything in our sin nature fights against its joy and peace, and fragments it. So if we hope to have such a holistic lifestyle of worship, we must, ever and always, ask God to give it to us.

### PRAYER

Aim your prayers in this direction:

- Pray that God would tear down the walls in your people's lives that separate the worship that takes place on Sunday from the worship of Monday through Saturday.
- Ask God for the gift of an increasingly God-fearing life, and for the Holy Spirit to open your people's eyes to see their lives in the world as locations for worship.
- Pray that the powerful patterns of worship—particularly the patterns of repentance—would shape the identities of your people, both in the upcoming service and over the years.

# 37 | Shalom Worship

### SCRIPTURE

*Read Isaiah 66:12–14.*

### DEVOTION

Many Bible commentators explain that the Hebrew word *shalom* is loaded with meaning. Because it often gets translated "peace," as it does here in this glorious prophecy from Isaiah, English speakers can be lulled by the false idea that shalom is simply something like inner calm or tranquility. But when you look at the word as it sweeps across Scripture, shalom means something far deeper: wholeness and integration, both of the personal kind and the cosmic kind. For now, let's talk about the relationship of shalom to us as individual worshipers.

As a worshiper, to be someone who experiences God's shalom is to be a person marked by a consistency, or integration, between our various "parts." Modern people speak of holistic health: addressing our wellness from all angles—mental, physical, spiritual, emotional, social, and so on. To worship in God's shalom—to be a mature worshiper—is to understand our worship life in a similar fashion to holistic health. It is to recognize that when I engage in a worship service with God's people, maturity will be marked by an integrated participation of all my different faculties—my mind, my will, my affections, and my body. All of me will be rowing in the same direction as I worship.

It's worthy of real lamentation that the twenty-first-century church is divided not only along doctrinal lines but also by how we express our worship. In a way, our various denominations and traditions express an incomplete portion of the universal church's integrated whole. Some traditions are known for outward and visible emotional expressiveness but maybe lack intellectual engagement. Other traditions emphasize thoughtfulness but might have more subdued physical expression. Some traditions worship in social ways, emphasizing horizontal connectivity with others. Some are personal and individualized, emphasizing strong vertical engagement with God from the heart.

Shalom reverses the outward forces that fragment us. God's promised kingdom of peace and wholeness calls to us from the future creating a gravitational pull, drawing us together around the throne of the Lamb. Worship is a chance to strain toward that future shalom by striving for an integration of self—body, mind, and soul, surrendered and poured out—and an integration of community—every kind of person joyfully aware of everyone else, eager to enact that intimate connectivity through love and shared rituals of song, prayer, posture, and heart.

Shalom beckons us to try uncomfortable things in worship, especially when we recognize those uncomfortable things as healthy for us or as a blessing to our neighbors. For those who feel reserved physically, shalom urges us to move our bodies, engage our arms, bend our knees, stretch out our hands. For those who feel disengaged intellectually, shalom urges thoughtfulness in pondering the depths of God's character, attributes, and deeds as we worship, eagerly integrating the revelation of biblical truth with the act of praise. For those who feel emotionally detached, shalom urges us to feel deeply, pressing in to all the light and dark hues of the affective spectrum.

Shalom calls us to more, not less; to integrity, not fragmentation; to intensification, not dulling. It calls creation together. It calls the Christian community together. It calls our divided selves together.

It's telling that when the angelic praise of heaven broke onto the ears of the shepherds before the first Christmas, they sang that his arrival would bring shalom on earth: "Glory to God in the highest, and on earth peace among those with whom he is pleased!" (Luke 2:14). This declaration that Jesus is shalom's center is all over Scripture. Isaiah prophesied that Jesus' "chastisement . . . brought us peace" (Isa. 53:5). Paul agreed that Jesus is "making peace by the blood of his cross" (Col. 1:20).

We have a glorious opportunity, a gracious invitation, to embody this shalom of the gospel in the way we worship. Perhaps that means that, for some of us, there might be some joyful discomfort to step into—some way we can make an effort toward that future wholeness now. And in any areas in which we feel we lack, the Spirit is eager to provide for the one who asks.

 **PRAYER**

Aim your prayers in this direction:

- Pray boldly for God's kingdom to come, specifically for foretastes, experiences, and expressions of the future shalom we will all share in Christ.
- Confess for yourself and on behalf of your worshiping community the lack of wholeness and completion in the way you worship now.
- Ask for a greater measure of strength and power from the Holy Spirit to engage in practices, expressions, and human faculties that are lacking or underserved in your life or in the life of your worshiping community.

# 38 | Bezalel and Oholiab

*Read Exodus 31:1–11.*

 DEVOTION

There are some passages of Scripture where, after reading, you just stop, look up at heaven, and say, "Thank you, God, that you put that in there!" For artists, this is that passage. There is something affirming and dignifying when we hear about God's concern for the craftsmanship and artistry involved in setting aside Bezalel and Oholiab for ministry.

Yes, I said ministry.

We tend to spiritualize ministry, like some of us tend to spiritualize worship. Because our worship involves immaterial, spiritual reality, and because the God we worship is unseen, we can fall prey to the idea that it's only the immaterial things that matter—or at least that are most important. Because we're prone to idolatrously abuse physical objects, buildings, technologies, and all the other stuff of worship, we double down on the spiritual nature of worship.

But we need to remember, God cares about the physical world. When he created it, he called it good, and when he created us, he said we were very good (Genesis 1). After the fall of Adam and Eve, God responded by becoming flesh and dwelling among us (John 1:14). And when Jesus rose from the dead, he had a glorified physical body, becoming the firstfruits for all of us, to show us that all of our selves—including our physical bodies—will be rebuilt for eternal life (1 Cor. 15:20–23).

So we mustn't spiritualize worship too much. Worship should

be as physical as it is spiritual, which means that ministry is physical too. Our passage here in Exodus 31 shows us that God attributes dignity to the artistic technologies around us, employed to beautify and intensify the worship experience by gripping our senses of sight, sound, touch, taste, and smell. No, this doesn't mean that we utilize these artistic technologies haphazardly or uncritically. If you read on in Exodus and in the other books after it, God provides artistic specifications to avoid pollution by the surrounding culture's idolatry.

But make no mistake—Bezalel and Oholiab were ministers set apart to make worship beautiful and compelling, to make it a feast for the affections. Artists were so important to God's plan that our passage says that God did something in those days he only otherwise did for prophets, priests, and kings. God said about Bezalel, "I have filled him with the Spirit of God" (Ex. 31:3). Yes, when you experience artistry in worship, you are experiencing the fruit of the Holy Spirit, the third person of the Trinity.

Churches should be robustly creative places. The obvious creativity we should honor and enjoy includes music, architecture, and the beautiful items adorning and accompanying our spaces—communion tables and vessels, baptismal fonts and pools, pulpits, paintings, stained glass, graphic design, projected images and backdrops, and, for more liturgically oriented churches, vestments and materials that signal the season of the church calendar.

Worshiping God should include observing and absorbing these things, knowing that the Spirit has empowered our sisters and brothers to create them. The Holy Spirit therefore intends to use them to speak to us. As we see our spaces, hear our music, touch our chairs, pews, and kneelers, and taste and smell the communion bread and wine, we allow all these multisensory means to be ways to hear God speak to us.

And finally, we also seek to give thanks for God's gifts of artistry among us, perhaps by making that gratitude tangible. Maybe this week, maybe today, we can go out of our way to thank one of the artists among us—to exercise one of the horizontal dimensions of worship where we glorify God by offering thankfulness from our hearts to someone else in Jesus' name (Col. 3:16–17).

### ⤳ PRAYER

Aim your prayers in this direction:

- Offer up special thanks for specific artists in your community who have contributed to worship's beauty and power.
- Ask the Holy Spirit to give your worshiping community a deeper and more powerful experience by opening up your senses to receive rich communication through artistry.
- Pray specifically for vocational artists and other artists who draw some of their livelihood from their art-making, that God would faithfully provide for all their needs and encourage them that their work is dignified, important, and valuable.

# 39 | Hearing Aids for the Gospel

 SCRIPTURE

*Read Galatians 1:3–9.*

## DEVOTION

Paul wrote a lot of letters to a lot of churches. Paul's letter to the Galatians is the only one where he comes right out of the gate with major criticism. He obviously has something on his mind, and he refrains from the usual niceties and affirmations that characterize his other letters. And what is he so fired up about?

Paul is concerned about the one thing he is always concerned about: the gospel. He's fiercely protective of the clarity of the good news of Jesus Christ. He wants no ambiguity about the church's central message and reason for existence—to receive and proclaim that Jesus came to do what we could never do for ourselves.

Paul goes on in the letter to the Galatians to rebuke the way they've compromised and made the good news of Jesus ambiguous. His charge is that they've sent mixed messages through their actions, which effectively have communicated, "God requires something of you before he will give Jesus to you."

Because our hearts are deceitful (Jer. 17:9) and because the flesh hates the Holy Spirit and his freeing gospel (Gal. 5:17–24; 2 Cor. 3:17), Christian worship is ever and always in danger of shrinking back from that clear word and of sending the anti-gospel and anti-Christ message that we must give something to God before he gives Jesus to us.

The Scriptures say unashamedly that the gospel is "the power of God" (Rom. 1:16). The apostle John records that when Jesus commissioned his disciples, he breathed on them the powerful

Holy Spirit to announce the freeing news of the gospel: "Receive the Holy Spirit. If you forgive the sins of any, they are forgiven them" (John 20:22–23).

Powerful, Spirit-filled worship, therefore, is gospel-centered worship. If we want the Spirit to fall like he did at Jesus' baptism, we need to declare the same glorious truth that the Father declared there: "Look at Jesus, the Son of God, in whom the Father is well pleased" (Matt. 3:17).

I'll offer a metaphor given me by a friend that both helps us to evaluate the clarity of the gospel in our gathered worship services and assists us in being attuned to it more regularly as we sing, pray, listen, and receive each week. The metaphor is this: everything in worship should function like a hearing aid for the gospel.

Just as hearing aids help those who are hard of hearing to listen with clarity, so every aspect of worship—from its elements, to its order, to its artistic surroundings—should assist us in hearing the good news of Jesus clearly. Paul says that "faith comes from hearing" (Rom. 10:17), and in a way, we can "hear" the gospel through all five of our senses.

Does this sermon help me to hear God's good news? Do our rituals and actions assist me in receiving Christ's work more clearly? Do these songs encourage me to depend less on myself and what I can do for God—do they drive me to confession, surrender, and need? Do I tend to be fixated on the stuff of worship—the beauty and power of the technology, vestments, vessels, and worship space—or does the stuff help me fix my eyes on Jesus, "the founder and perfecter of our faith" (Heb. 12:2)? When I come to worship, do I come with the expectation that God's agenda is to do two things: to show us our need for Jesus, and to give Jesus to us?

As we approach the worship service, we have a chance to perk up the ears of faith. We come with one prayer: "Holy Spirit, make Jesus more beautiful and believable to me this week than last week; give me ears to hear Christ and only him." And after we pray, we can approach worship together with confidence that God will put those hearing aids in our ears and give us Jesus, loud and clear.

 **PRAYER**

Aim your prayers in this direction:

- Pray for those in charge of leading and planning your church's weekly worship services. Ask the Lord to give them wisdom and discernment about the clarity of the gospel in worship.
- Pray that the Holy Spirit would magnify the good news of Jesus to every heart and mind in worship.
- Pray against the enemies of the gospel—the world, the flesh, and the devil—so that all distractions from and competition with the gospel might be eliminated.

# 40 | You're Really Getting Married

### ⇒ SCRIPTURE

*Read Revelation 19:6–9.*

### ⇒ DEVOTION

One of the metaphors God uses over and over again for his relationship to his people is the metaphor of marriage. It's present even in creation, when God makes man and woman in his image (Gen. 1:27). As Adam and Eve are bonded in marriage, their togetherness and union reflect God's own self-unity. Three persons, one God—two people, one flesh.

But human marriage doesn't just mirror God's intimate, triune, relational oneness. It describes just how deep God's relationship is with us. Ezekiel 16 records in pretty graphic detail how God pursued us, his bride, like an obsessed lover who won't accept no for an answer. When God expresses his deepest hurt at Israel's rebellion against him, he accuses her of being a cheating spouse (Hos. 4:15; Jer. 3:1–5). And when God promises to restore Israel, he uses the language of a failed marriage reconciled by a faithful bridegroom (Isa. 62:4–5).

Revelation tells us, though, that this is all more than a metaphor. Revelation records that on the day when Christ returns and ushers in his kingdom fully and finally, the event that consummates it all will be a wedding. It is called "the marriage of the Lamb" (Rev. 19:7), where Jesus finally receives his bride—us, the church.

Working backward from Jesus' second coming, we could say that Jesus' first coming—his inauguration of his kingdom—was a betrothal. Christ's first advent, we could say, was his engagement event, when he got down on one knee, slid a ring on our finger, and said, "You're the only one for me. I promise myself to you forever. This is my pledge. We *will* get married. No turning back for me."

This isn't stretching the text, by the way. Jesus employed the prophets' marriage language to refer to himself and us. Jesus referred to himself as our bridegroom more than once (Matt. 9:15; 25:1–13). When Jesus came, we got engaged.

Still, we've all seen it happen. Engaged couples, once confident on the night of the proposal, get cold feet a few months later. "Does he really love me? Do I really love him? Will this be forever?" And isn't that an apt description of the way it works in our relationship with God? As we wait for our wedding day, we experience doubt, distance, questioning. And yes, though engaged, we cheat on him too. "Maybe I should call it off," we think. Or, even more serious, "Why would he want me? I'm such a mess. Maybe he should call it off."

This moment right here—the place of doubt and wavering—is where we need to talk about weekly worship. A worship service, among other things, is where Jesus comes to his doubting, wandering, wavering bride and says, "I really do love you, and nothing you do could ever change that." A worship service is the place where Jesus reminds his bride that we really are engaged, and that he accepts full responsibility for seeing it through to the wedding day.

In this respect, it's unlike any other engagement we've ever known. All other engagements are held together by mutual commitment. But Jesus' engagement to us is unilateral. Remember, he went to that cross alone. He went all in alone. He signed his engagement contract in blood. This one-way, "never going to let you go" love is exactly what Paul was thinking about when he wrote, "For I am sure that neither death nor life, nor angels nor rulers, nor things present nor things to come, nor powers, nor height nor depth, nor anything else in all creation, will be able to separate us from the love of God in Christ Jesus our Lord" (Rom. 8:38–39).

Know that as you come to worship this week, Jesus' agenda is to grab you by the hands, press on that engagement ring, and look you in the eyes and say, "Yes, I really do love you. Yes, my promises are real." Or in the words of our passage in Revelation, which punctuate what we may be tempted to think is fantasy, "These are the true words of God" (Rev. 19:9).

With promises like that, why would we ever not want to come to worship?

 **PRAYER**

Aim your prayers in this direction:

- Pray for those who are wavering in their faith, questioning God, or doubting his love. Pray that God's love in Christ would not only be clearly preached in sermon, song, prayers, and sacrament but also be felt as comfort.
- Pray for those who feel a strong sense of guilt and shame this week, that they would know that God's mercy triumphs over judgment, and that he is gracious, compassionate, and mighty to save.
- Pray for people who come to worship this week who do not know Jesus. Pray that the pursuing love of the Holy Spirit would move in power in their hearts.

# 41 | Symbiotic Worship

## SCRIPTURE

*Read Amos 5:18–24.*

## DEVOTION

This is a strong passage, isn't it? Amos is calling out Israel's own form of an age-old problem. It's what we today might call "cultural Christianity"—religion that pays lip service to God, obeys God in outward form, worships God the way he has commanded, and yet it doesn't translate into action in the Christian life.

Israel's problem, according to Amos, was that they were worshiping God in all the right ways, but they didn't connect that with daily worship that looks like God's just kingdom—caring for the poor, sharing wealth freely and generously, dealing honestly with others (Amos 5:11–13).

There's a principle here about worship that runs right through the Bible: there is a symbiotic relationship between public worship on Sunday, and whole-life worship Monday through Saturday. Symbiotic—that's a big word. It's a biological term used to describe two organisms in nature that need each other to exist. Think of bees and flowers. The bee needs the flower's pollen to make nourishing honey and feed its young. The flower needs the bee's frequent visits to spread its pollen to other flowers and successfully reproduce and spread. Take one out of the ecosystem, and the other dies off quickly.

So it is with worship, Amos says. If worshiping God in your daily life is a sham, you can expect your experiences in gathered worship to shrivel into lifeless, hollow shells. We can pull out at least four ideas from worship's symbiotic character:

First, we learn that to neglect one is to neglect the other. If I don't make a habit of attending and engaging in public worship, I can expect that my daily life will struggle to be worshipful as well. As one symbiotic organism of worship goes dormant, the other one loses its energy and life.

Second, on the more positive side, to cultivate one helps to cultivate the other. If I make a habit of seeking God's glory in all of my life, and certainly if I seek to find times both alone and with others to worship the Lord through prayer and praise throughout the week, my experiences of worship on Sunday will also be enriched. Worshiping with God's people will become less laborious and more free. It will be less distracted and more engaged. Seeing and savoring God will be more natural. You could liken this to an athlete who understands the relationship between practice and game day. Practice gives you the repetitions so that the game-day flow is nearly automatic. Similarly, whole-life worship gives you the reps for Sunday, and Sunday's rhythms give you the reps for the week.

Third, the gospel must be central in our whole-life worship *and* our gathered worship. If whole-life and weekly gathered worship are symbiotic, then to be gospel centered and repentance oriented should be a fundamental reality not only on Sunday but Monday through Saturday. If the gospel is something we need to receive over and over again, how could we possibly imagine that daily repentance wouldn't somehow translate into worship services whose journey, shape, and structure look like repentance too?

Fourth, we learn that gathered worship isn't an escape from life, it's the essence of life. Gathered worship shouldn't be a place where certain topics or issues are off limits. For instance, if I must struggle to glorify God in the way I engage and respond to politics in my everyday life, I should be able to find those same struggles present before the Lord with his people in worship.

There's something, too, about gathered worship that should help center me, define me, and ground me in what is central about being human.

Worship pulls us together in an integrated life—an existence marked by consistency of character before others and of relationship before God. And if you're like me, you're immediately drawn to all the ways you don't measure up to this high, holy calling. You're thinking of all the ways you haven't been faithful to seek God in worship 24-7. So we do the only thing we can do. We run to the cross for mercy, grace, and pardon. And we seek its power, through the Holy Spirit, to pursue this beautiful, whole life.

 **PRAYER**

Aim your prayers in this direction:

- Spend time in confession together: voice to God the sorrow and contrition of a life that is less than the ideals of the symbiotic worship life.
- Ask God to make you and your church more passionate so you can all be more driven to seek after bold and sincere participation in gathered worship and to follow his Spirit into daily worship as "living sacrifices" (Rom. 12:1).
- Pray for the Holy Spirit to use this week's worship service to do the deep, formative work of making you and your brothers and sisters into the likeness of Jesus.

# 42 | Beyond Us and Them

*Read Psalm 139:13–23.*

### DEVOTION

Some film commentators these days bemoan the postmodern takeover of ethics in movies. In yesteryear, they say, it was clear who the good guys and the bad guys were. Good and evil were set in black-and-white contrast. But now, movies tend to sit much more comfortably in the gray, leading the audience to see the complex flaws of a film's supposed heroes and sympathize with the plight of its supposed villains.

This graying of ethics in film reflects larger cultural shifts in how we think. We're a lot more nervous about calling someone or something evil. And many of us are now leerier of language that seems to create an us-versus-them dynamic. The Scriptures both challenge and affirm this state of affairs, and Psalm 139 displays this challenge and affirmation in high definition. And yes, this has to do with worship.

Songwriters love Psalm 139, at least up through verse 18. Up until that moment, we are given one of the most intimate and personal prayers a human being could pray to God: we are seen and known, inside and out; we can't escape his presence; in our mother's womb, he personally oversaw the multiplication of cells that led to the bodies we now have.

Then verse 19 screeches in: "Oh that you would slay the wicked, O God!" And thus begins a brief but explosive tirade against God's enemies, punctuated by, "I hate them with complete hatred; I count them my enemies" (v. 22).

Songwriters don't know what to do with this about-face. The tone seems to change from intimate comfort to forceful hate. This sudden switch is hard to capture musically. It makes you wonder what the original music to this psalm was like and how our spiritual mothers and fathers—the ancient Israelites—felt when they were singing it.

Commentators rightly point out that at least part of what's going on here is that when one feels such a deep intimacy with God as is expressed in this psalm, one's heart beats to the same rhythm as God's. You love what he loves, but you also hate what he hates. To know and be known by God includes sharing his grief and repugnance toward all forms of sin and brokenness. And there's certainly a lesson for worship even if we were to stop right here: if we are truly and intimately encountering the living God in worship, it will affect our ethics and morals Monday through Saturday.

If the psalm stopped with verse 22, at the peak of enemy hatred, we'd have reason to think that this black-and-white, us-versus-them paradigm is the end of it. But then we are ushered into the quiet postlude—another unexpected turn: "Search *me*, O God, and know *my* heart. . . . See if there be any grievous way in me" (vv. 23–24). Surprise. A confession.

The church is tempted, time and again, to take an us-versus-them posture toward the surrounding culture and watching world. "All the good is *in here*, and all the evil is *out there*." And though this psalm certainly challenges any ethical paradigm that blurs the line between good and evil, it also does what the living and active Word of God has been doing since the dawn of creation (Heb. 4:12–13). It cuts every last one of us to the heart, like the words of the prophet Nathan to David when David was trying to hide from his sin and act as though the problem was all out there. As the Word declares, so Nathan says to us, "*You* are the man!" (2 Sam. 12:7).

If worship doesn't take every last one of us to the place of "search me, O God," something is wrong. If the "dividing wall of hostility" (Eph. 2:14) between us and them is not somehow confronted and torn down by the Word of Jesus Christ—which simultaneously accuses us that we are sinners and frees us by the power of his forgiving cross—then we haven't really encountered God.

Just as Psalm 139 takes us through a journey of identifying and then obliterating the us-versus-them dynamic, so worship should have that same effect. It won't erase the line between good and evil, but it will place us all on the same side of it, on that same level ground at the foot of the cross, where we're all confessing, all crying out for mercy, and all seeking the wholeness and healing that can be found only in Jesus. May the Holy Spirit lead us there as we enter into worship.

 **PRAYER**

Aim your prayers in this direction:

- Pray that your church, through confession and repentance, would be marked by that culture which breaks down the "hostility" between "us" as good people and "them" as bad people.
- Pray that your encounter with God would be so rich and powerful that it would shape the morals and ethics of the people the other six days of the week.
- Pray for places and spaces in worship for people—both Christian and non-Christian—to truly and deeply confess their sins to God and know and hear clearly the forgiveness that God offers in Jesus Christ.

# 43 | Good Old-Fashioned Submission

## SCRIPTURE

*Read Psalm 2.*

## DEVOTION

*Submission* is one of those Bible words that has fallen into unpopularity, sometimes for good reasons. The word, and the various passages of Scripture in which it is found, have been utilized to justify all kinds of unbiblical, unloving action, from domineering, top-down church authority, to emotional manipulation, to abuse in the home. It makes sense that we are sensitive to this word.

Yet as a work of the Holy Spirit in us, submission is a beautiful thing—a sign of love, of selflessness, of honoring the other. Ephesians 5 urges us to be filled with the Spirit *by* submitting to one another out of reverence for Christ (Eph. 5:18, 21). It helps us to see that submission to one another is the opposite of the unilateral and domineering approach that many of us are rightly concerned about.

Psalm 2 speaks about submission of a different kind, and we need to be careful not to import our bad experiences of submission gone wrong on the human level onto the submission to which God calls the entire world.

Psalms 1 and 2 share a close relationship, such that many commentators encourage us to see them as a single unit and therefore a single-voiced preamble to the Psalms in general. Because the Psalms are the Bible's prayer book and anthology of God's top 150 approved worship songs for the church, we should pay close attention to Psalm 2 as not only a preamble for the book but also a significant voice in our understanding of worship.

Psalm 2 asks an aggressive, provocative question about the

violence and chaos of the world: "Why do the nations rage and the peoples plot in vain?" (Ps. 2:1). It offers us the picture of a God who confidently laughs at all foolish attempts by humans to assert their power and control. But God does more than laugh. "He will speak to them in his wrath, and terrify them in his fury" (v. 5).

This may sound mean, harsh, or vindictive, but if you've ever been the victim of a leader who abuses power, this statement rings in your ears as good news. And this good news in Psalm 2 is centered on the declaration of the way God will put all other bad authority in its place: through establishing the kingship of his Son. In its context, no doubt Israel would see this Son as their human king, especially King David. But Christians rightly see this as ultimately referring to Jesus.

The call to worship is strong. The Son is to be "kissed." "Kiss the Son, lest he be angry, and you perish in the way" (v. 12). This isn't the kiss of lovers. It's that of a servant kissing the feet of a master. Total submission.

Though this psalm is definitely a warning to world leaders who have little time for God and his Word, it's also a warning to you and me. The truth is that you and I have little kings and queens sitting like despots on the thrones of our hearts. These rulers are constantly looking for ways to live independently, out from under the gracious provision of a loving Father. These kings and queens are falling prey to the temptation of the serpent to doubt God's word and promises: "Did God *really* say . . . ?" (Gen. 3:1).

Worship is a check to the despotic tendencies of the human heart. It is a confrontation of our bent toward rugged individualism and arrogant independence, reminding us that we must pray, "*Thy* will be done." Submission, therefore, comes to worship with these kinds of postures:

- God, make me ready to confess even the things that I don't know about.

- God, make me ready to hear all your truth, not just the truth that I want to hear.
- God, give me a quiet spirit, a listening spirit.
- Tear down the arrogant or degrading self-talk in my head and replace it with your Word.
- Make me quick to listen and quick to respond to your promptings and leading.
- "Humble yourselves before the Lord, and he will exalt you" (James 4:10).

### PRAYER

Aim your prayers in this direction:

- Spend time praising God's awesome kingship, might, and power. Glorify his sovereignty. Marvel at his strength. Magnify his might. Honor Jesus as king and ruler at the right hand of God the Father.
- Pray for world leaders. Ask God to bring their hearts and minds into submission to God and his Word.
- Pray for your people: for humble and tender hearts, hearts ready to yield to God, his will, and his Word, hearts ready to lay down personal agendas and confess need.

# 44 | A Safe Space

## SCRIPTURE

*Read Psalm 27:1–6.*

## DEVOTION

We often fall prey to thinking that worship is so much less than it is, forgetting the multifaceted richness and manifold benefits that are waiting for us there. Here's one of those benefits.

Gathered worship is a safe space. It's a place where we are allowed to run and hide. And even as I say that, I recognize that worship's safety isn't always apparent. Especially if we've grown up in the church or spent years worshiping with God's people, there have probably been times when worship didn't feel safe. Perhaps a preacher abused the pulpit and one too many times turned the Word of God from a balm into a bludgeon. Perhaps gathered worship was a place of wounding hypocrisy, where people you worshiped alongside on Sunday treated you on Monday through Saturday with behavior that didn't line up with that worship.

And still, in the middle of this, God has the audacity to give us a psalm—a prayer, a worship song—that presses us to know and feel that worship is a safe space. The Psalms are filled with language that reminds us, over and over, that God is a refuge, that his presence feels like a protective fortress. How do we reconcile what is often many peoples' experience with this good word from the Lord?

First, let's make sure God's Word is saying what we think it's saying. Did you notice verses 4–6? They form literarily what they proclaim verbally. The middle verse, verse 5—the verse that sings "he will hide me in his shelter in the day of trouble"—is *surrounded* by worship. Verse 4 sings, longingly, "One thing have I asked of the

LORD, that will I seek after: that I may dwell in the house of the LORD all the days of my life." Verse 6 sings, confidently, "And now my head shall be lifted up . . . and I will offer in his tent sacrifices with shouts of joy; I will sing and make melody to the LORD." And buffered by worship's protective padding are you and me: sheltered by God in the day of trouble.

So something about being in God's house with other broken people hides me. And that leads us to the second point: What hides me isn't necessarily that I'm shielded from any and all hurt or harm. What hides me is Jesus himself.

In gathered worship, we're not always guaranteed that the brokenness of everyone around us won't inflict damage on us. We certainly need spaces that are safe enough, but a perfectly safe space, this side of eternity, is probably an illusion. The apostle Paul, for instance, recognized that around the worshiping community in Philippi, some preachers of the gospel abused their pulpits out of false motives, out of "envy and rivalry" and "selfish ambition" (Phil. 1:15, 17). He also chastised the Corinthian worshipers for alienating others through their selfishness and hypocrisy in gathered worship (1 Corinthians 14). So if the early church couldn't get it right, I don't suspect we will either.

But even though we're not guaranteed perfect safety in worship, we are given one who is perfectly safe: Jesus. The psalm is peppered with references and allusions to him. "The LORD is my light and my salvation," verse 1 says. Remember it was our Savior Jesus who said, "I am the light of the world" (John 8:12). We are sheltered from stormy waves of trouble, the psalm says, by being lifted "high upon a rock" (v. 5). Who else is the rock of the church but Jesus, the chief cornerstone (Matt. 21:42; Acts 4:11; Eph. 2:20; 1 Peter 2:6–7)?

The psalm asks rhetorical questions, and we all know the answer: "Whom shall I fear? . . . Of whom shall I be afraid?" (v. 1). The Scriptures remind us again and again that the Holy Spirit is given to us particularly so that his perfect love might cast out all fear (1 John 4:18) and the spirit of slavery to fear might give way to the Spirit of adoption into a protective household (Rom. 8:15–17). Jesus will never truly hurt us; even in painful trials, he is growing us, not destroying us. Jesus will never abuse us. He is "gentle and lowly in heart" (Matt. 11:29).

So, surrounded by broken people, we come to hear an unbroken Word. Even more, we come to receive *the* unbroken Word. Worship is a place where we are not only told about Jesus, we are given Jesus. We are given the same Christ in whom the martyrs of old found so much safety that they could face death unflinchingly. We are given the same Christ in whom Mary found so much confidence that she was able to sing her resistance of both the tyranny of monarchs and the judgmental gossip of her peers (Luke 1:46–56). We are given the same Christ who guarantees a true and final justice, a sure and everlasting peace, on the other side of all this chaos.

Jesus is our safe space. Let's pray for the Holy Spirit to come in power, make much of Jesus, and make worship a safe space.

 **PRAYER**

Aim your prayers in this direction:

- Pray specifically for people in your community who are suffering from the wounds of other Christians, who come to worship scarred or hanging on by a thread. Pray that God visits them tangibly and that they might receive and feel genuine love from others today.
- Pray that today's service, in particular, would offer words and feelings of comfort—that the Holy Spirit, the Comforter, would come in power to do what only he can do.
- Pray that those who are greeting and welcoming others into the service would be able to embody in their words and countenance the welcoming comfort of Jesus.

# 45 | Working Backward from the End

## SCRIPTURE

*Read Revelation 7:9–12.*

## DEVOTION

Christianity is all about working backward from the end. For example, in Romans 3 Paul tells us in no uncertain terms that because of what Jesus did for us on the cross, our future final judgment will be "not guilty." Christians rest secure because we have no fear of what will happen. Christ's finished work is our secure promise. This working backward from the end operates similarly in worship.

In Revelation, the apostle John describes visions he saw of the future. The vision we're looking at in chapter 7 is a vision of what future worship will be like. First, we see it's centered on Christ, both figuratively and literally. Everyone is "standing before the throne and before the Lamb" (v. 9). They're singing songs of worship *to* the Lamb (vv. 10, 12).

Second, we see that it's a *lot* of people: "A great multitude that no one could number" (v. 9). This means that heaven isn't going to be filled with a few of just the earth's elites. As the old hymn goes, "There's a wideness in God's mercy," and we're told to expect that loads and loads of people will all be there, purified and glorified around the throne because our God is gracious and merciful.

Third, we see multiethnic, multicultural diversity of the richest kind, in complete harmony. The vision says "from every nation" (v. 9). Every culture, every kind of human being will be represented. There will be full mutuality, equality, and harmony. There will be no stratifications, no class distinctions, no racism.

There will be a celebration of Jesus through the diverse display of the image of God, visible in the beauty of every kind of face, body, skin tone, and language. Eyes of all different shapes and colors will be mesmerized by the overwhelming beauty of the Lamb. Hair of all different hues, lengths, and textures will be blown back by the awesome shock wave of glory bursting from Jesus' throne.

Christ centered. Innumerable. Multicultural. Christians, that is future worship. And now we have a joyful and challenging question before us: If that is the future toward which God is taking our worship, how might we press into that future here and now? What's the difference between that future reality and our present reality, and how can we attempt to close that gap with all joy and thanksgiving? How can we work our way backward from the future?

Future worship is Christ centered. How can we center more of our worship on Jesus and his work for us in his life, death, and resurrection? How can our songs, prayers, preaching, and celebration of the Lord's Supper and baptism all increase in fixing our eyes on the author and perfecter of our faith (Heb. 12:2)? How can we more richly confess and lament our sin and our world's brokenness, so that all of that darkness provides the starkest backdrop against which the Light of the World can shine?

Future worship gathers innumerable masses of redeemed people. What does it mean to press toward the worship of multitudes, especially when many of our churches are smaller, humbler gatherings of people? Certainly, this fact challenges us that the mission of the church to preach the gospel to every nation is important. This vision of future worship drives our mission: heavenly worship will be bigger, so let's go be a part of what God is doing and gather them in! It's also a reminder that when we worship in our small communities, we are worshiping with all the other small communities gathered in their spaces across the globe. We don't worship just with the people we see, and that's encouraging.

Future worship is multicultural. What does it mean to press toward multicultural worship? The simplest way is to ask ourselves, "What's the next step we can take to broaden ourselves beyond our cultural borders?" Sometimes that step isn't even a shift or change in your worship service. In fact, that shouldn't be the first step. The first step is always relationship. How can we aim for the future by expanding our relational boundaries, making room for friendship with and listening to people who are different from us? You will find that when those relational connections increase, the worship growth just might happen a bit more naturally.

Wherever your church is now, this vision should feel less like a burden and more like an invitation. This is where we're headed, church. And it's beautiful, but it's no small task. It's a challenge we're actually not up to facing. It's God sized. So, as with everything, we need to surrender our projects, return to God in dependent faith, and ask him to do what only he can do.

 **PRAYER**

Aim your prayers in this direction:

- Pray that the Holy Spirit would seize you and your church with this vision of the future in Revelation 7. Ask God to give you a hunger to see these realities here and now.
- Pray that the Holy Spirit would reveal to your church community the simple next steps you can take to move toward this future vision.
- Pray that God would open up your church relationally to make new, meaningful connections with different kinds of people, for the sake of the mission of God in gathering the nations in.

# 46 | The Wilderness of Worship

## SCRIPTURE

*Read Matthew 3:1–6.*

## DEVOTION

Many modern social theorists tell us that our connected and tech-nologized society is perhaps the loneliest of any generation. We may have more friends and followers on social media, but our sense of isolation just might be at an all-time high. The Scriptures address this feeling.

It's telling that Jesus' ministry begins with a herald—John the Baptist—who blazes the trail for the Savior of the world not in the city center but, as the text says, "in the wilderness of Judea" (Matt. 3:1). In the original language, this word, "wilderness," is a dark and des-perate word. It's actually an adjective: isolated, desolate, deserted. This lonely word is the word Paul uses to describe Jerusalem as a woman who is single and infertile—she has neither the companion-ship of a husband by her side nor of a child in her belly (Gal. 4:27).

And John the Baptist goes to *that* place to announce Jesus' coming. The wilderness is a major motif in the redemption story of the Bible. It is where Jacob "was left alone" to wrestle with God and receive the name Israel (Gen. 32:22–32). It is the place where the Israelites wandered for forty years (Josh. 5:6). It is where, before his kingship, a desperate David had to hide to escape Saul's sword (1 Sam. 23:24). And it is the place where Jesus eventually went as our substitute to do lonely battle with the devil for forty days and nights (Matt. 4:1–11).

It's an unlikely yet beautiful comfort, then, given how much wilderness is in the Bible and how much wilderness is in our lives, that Jesus' ministry starts there. Wilderness, in Israel's mind, is the place of both judgment and renewal. It's the place where God calls out the Israelites for rebelling and not living up to who he is and what he has called them to be. But it's also the place, on the other side of that accusation, loneliness, and humbling, where they are renewed, brought out, and restored to intimate relationship with God in the promised land.

Do you hear all the overtones for worship? Worship always begins with God meeting the lonely ones in the wilderness. Wilderness is built into the physical experience of worship, isn't it? We all come from our separate, isolated living quarters. We walk, ride, or drive to a certain place, and we come *together*. We bring all our wildernesses with us—our broken relationships, our stressful jobs, our pressured work and living environments—and God meets us together in that place.

And what happens in the wilderness must also happen to us in worship. We experience the progression from judgment to renewal. The wildernesses we bring express the reality that we are contributors to the lonely mess we're in—from our isolating, screen-centered addictions, to our repelling self-righteousness and self-centered behavior. To that wilderness, the Word of God comes and says repent. Every good worship service calls us to repentance. In fact, the only way out of this wilderness is through repentance.

But good worship also brings us face to face in an encounter with the God who is, as the Scriptures say over and over again, "merciful and gracious, slow to anger and abounding in steadfast love" (Ps. 103:8). This is the description of God that Moses hears when he is in the wilderness of Sinai receiving the tablets of the Law (Ex. 34:6). The wilderness is *where* God shows himself to be gentle and merciful.

So, too, worship will be a place where that word of comfort reaches its climax in God's "I forgive you" and "I love you" in Jesus

Christ—where our loneliness and isolation are addressed in the Word of Christ, which gathers us in to find rich communion with God and with others. Worship presents to us a foretaste of the kingdom of God—a wilderness-less future where everyone is harmoniously connected to God and to one another and where no one ever feels alone. So we come to worship this week with great hope. And we stand beside John the Baptist, there in our wildernesses, with great expectation that God will come to us in Jesus, by the power of the Spirit.

 **PRAYER**

Aim your prayers in this direction:

- Pray specifically for those in your church and surrounding community who feel the weight of loneliness and isolation. Pray God's Spirit would bring them to worship with God's people.
- Pray that the Spirit would make clear the necessary two-part journey we all must take in worship: from judgment to renewal. Pray that the service would open up that pathway for every person.
- Pray that God's "I love you" in Jesus would be the loudest and most lasting thing people receive and take away from the time together.

# 47 | Worshiping "Before the Gods"

### SCRIPTURE

*Read Psalm 138:1–6.*

### DEVOTION

There's a lot of talk about trying to make the worship environment comfortable for people. I get the idea. The apostle Paul encouraged the Corinthian Christians, against selfishness, to make worship hospitable to outsiders. It shouldn't be hard for someone who doesn't know Jesus to understand what's going on, Paul argued (1 Cor. 14:23–25). Still, I don't know whether comfortable is the right word to describe the hospitality of worship. Understandable? Certainly. Convicting? Hopefully. Comfortable? Not quite.

When Paul describes what the non-Christian's experience should be like, he describes it as being "convicted by all" and "called to account" because "the secrets of his heart are disclosed" (vv. 24–25). This doesn't sound like a comfortable experience to me.

We get those same discomforting vibes from the psalmist's strange phrase "before the gods I sing your praise" (Ps. 138:1). Before the gods? Yes, it's a little odd to be thinking about worshiping the true and living God in front of other gods. Why even make mention of it? Doesn't the Bible teach that "an idol has no real existence" and that there is only one real God (1 Cor. 8:4)? True enough, and yet we all know that though the gods aren't real, they certainly exert a strong influence over humanity. The problem with the gods isn't the gods themselves but what human hearts make of them.

And here's probably where we're tempted to slip into the

us-versus-them fallacy. The gods, really, are a problem for *those* people—you know, those people who don't know God, or at least don't know God like *I* know him. But this is where God's Word comes in like a hammer: "For the word of God is living and active, sharper than any two-edged sword . . . discerning the thoughts and intentions of the heart. And no creature is hidden from his sight, but all are naked and exposed to the eyes of him to whom we must give account" (Heb. 4:12–13).

If the living and active Word is present in a worship service, you'd better believe that you're worshiping not just before *the* gods, you're worshiping before *your* gods. Are you uncomfortable yet?

For the Christian, to worship "before the gods" is always a two-step process. You can't have the euphoria without first having the exposure. You can't have the praise without the pulverizing. You can't have the comfort without the conviction. You can't have the resurrection without the death. If I want, as the psalm says, to give thanks to the Lord "with my *whole* heart," my gods must be called to account. I can't worship around my gods. I can't worship alongside my gods. I must be ready for the confrontation of worshiping *before* my gods.

There's an ancient Latin prayer that made its way into English-speaking worship services at the time of the Reformation. Most Anglicans know it by heart because it's one of the first things spoken in a communion service. It's a before-the-gods kind of prayer: "Almighty God, unto whom all hearts are open, all desires known, and from whom no secrets are hid: Cleanse the thoughts of our hearts by the inspiration of your Holy Spirit."

A god is anything that you or I deem ultimate. For many of us, an idol is formed in our hearts when we make a good thing an ultimate thing—the thing that drives our allegiance and affections, the thing that would undo us if we lost it. It's the thing we wake up thinking about or the thing we go to bed unable to get out of our minds and hearts.

When we really worship God, all those other gods are forced into public shame because they can't offer what we often believe they promise. They can't offer deep peace or lasting joy. They can't deliver the steadfast love and faithfulness that God can. They can't be there for us when we're falling apart, and they can't offer new strength and new mercies when we're weak and we blow it.

So each week, a worship service is a place to get freshly sobered up and knocked back into reality: God is God, and our gods are worthless. No wonder God wants us to worship weekly; the gods are always before us, and they always need fresh confrontation. It's serious business, so let's pray for God to come in power, but let's also pray for grace and mercy to withstand it so we can find our faithful Savior on the other side.

 **PRAYER**

Aim your prayers in this direction:

- Pray for the Holy Spirit to come in convicting power (John 16:8) but also in the comfort of the gospel (Rom. 8:14–17).
- Pray that worship would be a safe place for people to feel honest before God.
- Pray for your church leaders to be able to model honesty before God, both inside and outside the worship services.
- Pray for non-Christians who are present, that God would meet them in power.

# 48 | Digging for His Presence

*Read Isaiah 57:14–15.*

 DEVOTION

God's presence is the foundation of worship. If God is not present, our worship is in vain. Our rituals are hollow. Our prayers hit the ceiling. Our songs don't reverberate. Our preaching is mute.

But Scripture tells us that when God is present, many things are true. Just surveying the Psalms shows us that the following things happen when God is present: God's enemies flee (Ps. 9:3), we feel sheltered and protected (Ps. 31:20), justice breaks out (Ps. 17:2), the earth trembles (Ps. 114:7), our sin is exposed so it can be dealt with (Ps. 90:8), we experience "pleasures" and "fullness of joy" (Pss. 16:11; 21:6), and singing uncontrollably bursts forth (Ps. 100:2).

God's presence is awe inspiring. It takes us to the extreme edges of our emotions. In the presence of God, we experience the spectrum of emotion, from deep fear to unspeakable comfort. It's the most powerful experience we could have. Imagine the most amazing concert you've ever attended, the most inspiring talk you've ever heard, the most mindblowing movie you've ever watched, or the most exhilarating theme park you've ever been to. Think of the most fully immersive experience you've ever had.

And now multiply that experience by infinity. That gets you a bit closer to what the Bible describes as the unfiltered experience of God's awesome presence.

Oh, how we long for worship to feel like that. But we tend to encounter only glimpses, foretastes, and fleeting moments punctuating by long stretches of mediocrity. Even so, we're urged by Scripture to "seek the Lord and his strength; seek his presence continually!" (Ps. 105:4). An immediate question arises: Where do I find God's presence? Or to use some parallel scriptural language, Where does God dwell?

One answer to this question is found in our passage in Isaiah. And in this instance, God dwells in an unexpected place. The context of Isaiah's prophecy is important to feeling the gravity of the verses here. Almost like a hurt lover, embittered by the betrayal of his people, God lays it on strong in Isaiah 57. He chastises Israel for absolutely horrible things—things like sexual promiscuity and murdering children (Isa. 57:5, 8).

From the way God is saying all these things, you get the mounting feeling that God is about to unload. But right at the moment when you think the cup of wrath is going to overflow, our verses come in:

> Thus says the One who is high and lifted up,
>     who inhabits eternity, whose name is Holy:
> "I dwell in the high and holy place,
>     and also with him who is of a contrite and lowly
>         spirit,
> to revive the spirit of the lowly,
>     and to revive the heart of the contrite."
>
> —Isaiah 57:15

We learn something about God's character here in the way he uses his threatening Word in leading up to this moment of tender grace. Even as he rains down truthful accusations, he is not willing that any should perish (2 Peter 3:9). He unleashes his wrath for a purpose: to break our hard hearts, to crack us open, to deliver us from stubborn defiance to submissive dependence. Consistent with his good character, God's wrath, as always, is an agent of his love.

Here's the crazy thing. *That* place. That place right there, where we're broken open, is the place where Isaiah tells us that God dwells. God is "with him who is of a contrite and lowly spirit." In this instance, God isn't found in the high places. He's found in the low spots. We don't climb up to find God. We find him when we fall down. He's found in the valley as much as he is found on the mountaintop.

And that's good news for sinners like you and like me. It means that as we come to worship, we can start digging deep into our hearts to unearth all the hidden brokenness, shame, and guilt that we've buried there. Because, as it turns out, when we dig deep in those locations, we won't just find our sin. In Christ, we find God present there—forgiving, loving, and healing. So pick up your shovels, worshipers.

 **PRAYER**

Aim your prayers in this direction:

- Ask the Holy Spirit to send forth the mighty, living, and active Word of God to soften hard hearts that are resisting God's nearness and love.
- Ask the Holy Spirit to send forth the tender, living, and active Word of God to comfort the tender consciences and weak spirits who feel like they are too far from God to be loved and brought back.
- Pray for a powerful time of confession to break open in worship this week.

# 49 | Easily Blessed

*Read 1 Thessalonians 5:16–18.*

### DEVOTION

Chip Stam, a professor of worship who is now with the Lord, was well known in his circles for a saying that goes something like this: "The mature Christian is one who is easily blessed." When I first heard that statement, I didn't like it.

Being someone who has been in and around churches and church culture my whole life, I know what a person looks like who is "easily blessed." To me, the easily blessed person seems naive, a little too ignorantly happy about everything. In my mind, the easily blessed person has their head in the sand and doesn't see that difficulty and suffering are real and that the Christian life involves struggle. But the older I get, the more I realize that Dr. Stam was exactly right. To be easily blessed is to be someone who lives out Paul's words to the Thessalonians to "give thanks in all circumstances" (1 Thess. 5:18).

Over and over again, the Scriptures characterize the Christian life with a single word: thankfulness. Even more, two of the most important New Testament passages on worshiping through music highlight thanksgiving as a chief feature of the gathered time together. Ephesians 5 says that "giving thanks always" is the outworking of being filled with the Spirit in public worship (Eph. 5:18–20). Colossians 3 encourages us that thankfulness is a telltale sign that the Word of Christ is dwelling in us richly (Col. 3:16). Thanksgiving is what our lives look like when we are worshiping in a Spirit-filled, Bible-saturated, Christ-centered way.

The reason that thanksgiving is so central to what it means to be a follower of Jesus is because the Christian understands that all of life, all the way down to the small things, is a gift from God. As Paul asks rhetorically, "What do you have that you did not receive?" (1 Cor. 4:7). In a sense, all of our deeds, from when we wake up to when we lay our heads down at night, are a response to God's faithful provision.

Even our sleeping is a gift from God, a place where we relinquish trying to "work hard for Jesus" and simply receive the gifts of the God who goes ahead of us. Psalm 127 sings, "It is in vain that you rise up early and go late to rest, eating the bread of anxious toil; for he gives to his beloved sleep" (v. 2). Rest is a gift from God. When we sleep, we don't cease experiencing God's gifts. We fall into yet more of them.

What characterizes the easily blessed life seems to be an ability to quickly recognize all the gifts that are coming at you on a daily, hourly, minute-by-minute basis. The thankful person is so busy recognizing all the wonderful provisions of the Lord that they simply don't have bandwidth for negativity. They lack a selfish and critical spirit simply because there's no room for such thoughts in the overflow of God's goodness. Thankfulness has filled them to the brim.

Worship services, lamentably, are places where critical spirits often work overtime. We take the consumer mentality shaped and emphasized by culture Monday through Saturday and drag it right on into Sunday morning. "I don't like this product." "This isn't what I want." "I'm not getting what I paid for." "This isn't giving me what I'd hoped." Consumerism, and the machinery of advertising that perpetuates it, shapes us to be people constantly evaluating whether we are completely satisfied. We often unknowingly bring those critical, self-focused lenses right into the service.

Instead of entering his gates with thanksgiving, we come with a checklist of demands that must be met. Instead of simply receiving straight into our hearts whatever gift God is giving to us in the worship service, we hold the gift at arm's length, turn it over, inspect it, critique it, judge it. Such a move spoils the gift and sours us.

Meanwhile, the easily blessed person to my left is full of joy, peace, goodness, patience. She's full of, well, the Spirit and his fruits (Gal. 5:22–23). When I look at her overflow, I recognize that she possesses a maturity I have yet to receive. Her life is a receptacle for the gifts of God, and the entry portal to that receptacle has no hatch, gate, or filter. Her life has become what God was attempting to shape Israel into when he said, "I am the LORD your God, who brought you up out of the land of Egypt. Open your mouth wide, and I will fill it" (Ps. 81:10).

I want that open, gift-filled, thankful life, don't you? I want the maturity of easy blessing, the joy of seeing God's good provision everywhere. Funny enough, that too is a gift. So why don't we simply ask for it, for ourselves and our people?

### ⤙ PRAYER

Aim your prayers in this direction:

- Pray that the Holy Spirit would challenge the consumeristic spirit of criticism and evaluation in your heart and in the hearts of your people.
- Ask the Holy Spirit to give you and your community eyes to see all the gifts God is giving daily.
- Pray for a Spirit of thankfulness to permeate the room in the upcoming worship service.

# 50 | So You Want to Encounter Jesus

*Read Luke 24:13–32 [for a shorter reading: Luke 24:13–16, 27–32].*

## DEVOTION

This story has worship written all over it. It opens to a scene after Jesus' resurrection when two dejected disciples are on a road between towns. They're headed away from Jerusalem. Even that geographical fact is significant. They're headed away from the city where God's presence was. Every good God-fearer knew that if you wanted to encounter God, Zion was the place to be. (See Ps. 132:13.) But these disciples were discouraged and defeated. They thought their leader was dead, and all their hopes were gone. God's presence, now fading behind them, seemed a distant memory.

But Jesus appears. And doesn't he always do this? He doesn't appear when we're ready, prayed up, or sold out. He appears when we least expect it, when our backs are turned to him, when we've given up, when all hope is lost. Or in Paul's words, he appears "while we were still sinners" (Rom. 5:8).

A careful reading of what follows gives us some significant clues that Luke intends for Christians to think about worship as they hear of how Jesus reveals himself to these downtrodden disciples. The first clue is in 24:27: "And beginning with Moses and all the Prophets, he interpreted to them in all the Scriptures the things concerning himself." A Christian worshiper recognizes this as the language of a significant event that should happen in every good worship service: preaching.

It hearkens back to the beginning of Luke when Jesus first

enters the public scene. If you have a red-letter Bible, this is when you first start seeing the red. Chapter 4 tells us that Jesus came to Nazareth, "and as was his custom, he went to the synagogue on the Sabbath day, and he stood up to read" (Luke 4:16). The day's reading was a prophecy from Isaiah 61, and when Jesus was done, he closed his Hebrew Bible and he began to preach. The essence of his sermon? "What you just heard was all about me."

This is what happens on the road to Emmaus. It says that as Jesus preaches the Hebrew Bible, he "interpreted to them . . . the things concerning himself." Jesus' first recorded postresurrection sermon is a Christ-centered message from the Old Testament.

But that's not all. After the sermon, they find themselves at a table, where Jesus "took the bread and blessed and broke it and gave it to them" (Luke 24:30). This sequence—taken, blessed, broken, given—is just the sequence a Christian worshiper is used to experiencing in worship when they receive the Lord's Supper. And it was during this moment of what we now call communion that the text says "their eyes were opened, and they recognized him" (v. 31). And after Jesus departed suddenly, they immediately thought back to Jesus' earlier sermon. Their comment was amazingly experiential: "Did not our hearts burn within us while he talked to us on the road, while he opened to us the Scriptures?" (v. 32).

The message for worship is clear. In our day and age, many of us are used to talking about having powerful worship experiences during music and singing. We use language like "I experienced God" or "we were burning with passion for the Lord" or "God's presence in the room was palpable." And without a doubt, the Scriptures affirm that we should expect to encounter God in our singing.

But here we have a different take. We actually get more than we often realize. Jesus comes at us in the power of the Holy Spirit not only in our singing but also when sermons are preached and when we gather around the Lord's table to eat bread and drink of the cup in Jesus' name. We can and do have powerful, Spirit-filled, experiential, heart-enflaming, overwhelming encounters with Jesus there too.

We should lean into these practices with expectation that God will be just as present in those places to touch us, speak to us, come to us, and change us. Therefore, this day, let's pray for that holy expectation for ourselves and our people as we prepare for worship.

 **PRAYER**

Aim your prayers in this direction:

- Pray for an Emmaus-like encounter—hearts on fire—for you and your people during the preaching of the Word.
- Pray that God would enliven the preaching of your church to be increasingly Christ centered and to interpret out of every passage of Scripture the person and work of Jesus.
- If you are celebrating communion this Sunday, pray expectant prayers and ask God to prepare the hearts of his people to encounter him there. If communion is happening on a future Sunday, begin praying now for that celebration and encounter in the same manner.

# 51 | Over the Chaos

 **SCRIPTURE**

*Read Psalm 29.*

 **DEVOTION**

"The voice of the LORD is over the waters" (Ps. 29:3). I don't know how that line strikes you, but the ancient Hebrew would have heard that statement as a comfort. Early Israel understood what many of us still identify with: the sea is a terrifying place. In the ancient world, the ocean was a frightful mystery—unknown creatures lived in it, spontaneous storms arose upon it, and brave seafarers were swallowed by it.

The waters represented chaos—a place of disorder and anarchy. So when Psalm 29 sings, "The voice of the LORD is over the waters," the people of God are making an anxiety-calming truth claim: "God stands as King over the chaos of my life."

The most terrified I've ever been was when I went surfing one morning with my friends on the south shore of Oahu, Hawaii, at a spot called Bowls. The sun hadn't risen and the ocean was black and foamy over the reef. We paddled out, I dropped into a wave, but I didn't catch it right. I lost my balance and fell into the base of the wave as it turned over. Though it was probably just fifteen seconds, it felt like two minutes of disorienting, oxygen-deprived panic. All surfers will tell you that it's useless to swim or struggle in that moment because the waters are so churned that they offer no grip, no swimming leverage, and no sense of gravity, up, or down. You just have to wait, cover your head, and then let it toss you and eventually spit you out.

In between Sundays, our week has a way of doing this, even

to the strongest of Christians. Monday through Saturday, we get tossed, battered, and churned. Whether it's a challenging relationship, tension at work, pressure at school, conflict at home, or the very real spiritual war against the world, the flesh, and the devil, we are all victims of the chaos we have participated in creating.

When we come to worship, we come to remember that "the voice of the Lord is over the waters." We come to be pulled out of the chaotic, churning waters and set down safely on the Rock of Ages. How does worship do this? Psalm 29 points us back to the beginning of time.

Genesis begins with these famous lines: "In the beginning, God created the heavens and the earth. The earth was without form and void, and darkness was over the face of the deep. And the Spirit of God was hovering over the face of the waters" (Gen. 1:1–2). Did you hear that? Psalm 29 borrows a lyrical line from the poetry of Genesis. We learn here that Psalm 29 understands "the voice of the Lord" to be the activity of the Holy Spirit.

In worship, it is the Holy Spirit who inhabits God's voice. The Spirit comes with the Word. When the Scriptures are sung, prayed, preached, and proclaimed at the table and at baptism, the Spirit comes to turn our chaos into order. Genesis tells this story in great detail, actually. Because once we hear of the Spirit hovering over the waters, God begins to declare his creative Word, "Let there be!"

When we come to worship, we come with our churning chaos in need of God's Spirit-filled "Let there be!" God says, "Let there be forgiveness!" "Let there be reconciliation!" "Let there be healing!" "Let there be justice!" "Let there be wholeness!" "Let there be calm!" "Let there be unity!" "Let there be joy!" "Let there be freedom!"

Interestingly, Psalm 29 sings for quite a while about the authority and power of God's Word before getting to any human response. But once it's time to respond, the psalm simply says in verse 9, "And in his temple all cry, 'Glory!'" The job of worshipers is simply to throw themselves into the act of worship, crying "Glory!" to God.

And what is the payoff of coming to worship, receiving the chaos-calming Word, and crying "Glory!" in response? The psalm ends this way: "May the LORD give strength to his people! May the LORD bless his people with peace!" Strength. Peace. Fortitude. Calm. The opposite of chaos.

Worship, if nothing else, is a place to be transferred each week from the churning waters of chaos into the safe harbor of peace, ever and always through the power of the Spirit-filled Word of God. So as we go to prayer, hear God's powerful Word to us: "Let there be peace."

### ⤳ PRAYER

Aim your prayers in this direction:

- Pray that God would address the chaos in the lives of your brothers and sisters as they enter into worship.
- Ask the Spirit to unleash the Scriptures to do a mighty work through all the different ways the Word of God goes forth in worship—song, prayer, sermon, and sacrament.
- Pray for a unified sense of peace to fall on the people of God at the end of the service before they go out into the world to live out God's mission in their various vocations.

# 52 | What Qualifies Us to Serve

*Read Psalm 51:1–13.*

 DEVOTION

What qualifies us all to serve in ministry? This question is important, and it receives a fair amount of attention in the New Testament. Before we answer that question, though, it's good for a gathered group of Christians who are preparing in various ways to help facilitate a worship service to understand what ministry is.

Some of us are tempted to believe that ministry is something that only pastors and church staff do. But if you're a Christian, the Bible considers you a minister. In Ephesians, when Paul is listing various roles in the church, he is quick to say that all those roles exist "to equip the saints for the work of ministry, for building up the body of Christ" (Eph. 4:12). This means that if you're a Christian, you've been given the Holy Spirit and his gifts so that you can minister to others. So no matter who you are today—whether you're a musician, a greeter, a sound engineer, a preacher, a communion preparer, or an usher—you've been called to minister in that role.

Your objective is to participate in your role in such a way that you are building other people up to look, smell, and act like Jesus. Don't shy away, then, from the opportunity to declare to your sisters and brothers the Word that has the power to build them up—the gospel. Remind them of who Jesus is and what he has done for them.

Now that we've established that you are indeed a minister, the question is before us: What qualifies you? We don't have a direct answer, but we can derive a few ideas from passages in 1 Timothy and Titus that address what is required of ministers known as elders or deacons. 1 Timothy 3 lists a series of virtues like "sober-minded," "able to teach," "not quarrelsome," "not double-tongued," and "not addicted to much wine." Titus 1 has a similarly intimidating list, capped off with this statement: "an overseer, as God's steward, must be above reproach" (Titus 1:7).

Though we're not all called to the roles outlined here, these qualifications cascade down to the rest of us who are all being equipped for ministry. And yes, if we're being honest, it should make us squirm. "Above reproach" . . . let it sink in. No doubt even as we were hearing that list of virtues some of us were thinking of the ways we haven't lived up to those qualifications.

This brings us to Psalm 51, written by a man called to a specific ministry in Israel's day: king. David was called to lead his people politically and administratively, but he was also called to lead spiritually and through his character. And he failed. He failed hard. He committed adultery, impregnating a woman who undoubtedly felt coerced by his powerful position, and he tried to cover it all up by having her husband murdered. (See 2 Samuel 11.) This is what we call today a moral failure.

Psalm 51 is David's confession, a worship song borne out of his failure. It's gritty and honest, full of contrition and brutal honesty. "My sin is ever before me," David weeps. "I was brought forth in iniquity," he admits. "Create in me a clean heart," he begs. And then something weird happens. It feels like an about-face, a sudden shift in direction.

Verse 13 seems to come out of nowhere. After wrapping up his confession with the desperate plea "restore to me the joy of your salvation," he moves into this odd statement: "*Then* I will teach transgressors your ways, and sinners will return to you."

"Teaching transgressors your ways" sounds like, well, ministry. We learn from Psalm 51 the surprising news that one of the preeminent qualifications for ministry is acquaintance with one's own sin and brokenness. Have you wondered whether you're fit to minister, fit to be among God's people and in his presence? Old-hymn writer Joseph Hart puts it this way:

> Let not conscience make you linger;
> Nor of fitness fondly dream.
> All the fitness he requireth
> Is to feel your need of him.

Do you feel your need of him today? Do you hunger and thirst for his righteousness because you're painfully aware of your lack of righteousness? God says, "That hunger is *the* essential qualification for faithful ministry." Ministry out of need is really the best—and only—kind of ministry there is. So as you prepare to minister, throw yourself wholly on Jesus again and let the Holy Spirit do the work of ministry in you and through you.

## ⤳ PRAYER

Aim your prayers in this direction:

- Spend some time confessing your sin. It doesn't have to be deeply personal or specific, and feel free to use the words of Psalm 51:1–12 to guide your language.
- Praise Jesus that he is our entry ticket and qualification; adore his righteous life and meritorious death on our behalf.
- Ask the Holy Spirit to embolden every ministry volunteer—and even every worshiper—to minister the gospel to one another before, during, and after the worship service.

# Conclusion

## *Passing the Baton*

The goal of *Before We Gather* is to establish a practice that shapes a culture. Especially if you've used this resource on a weekly basis throughout the year in a group format, I'm anticipating that you'll be able to see some differences in your services. Why am I so confident about that?

I want to borrow a bit from Paul, who said boldly, "I am not ashamed of the gospel, for it is the power of God for salvation" (Rom. 1:16). Similarly, I am not ashamed of prayer, because prayer is a Christian practice shaped like the gospel that creates it.

The gospel is the good news that in spite of ourselves (rather than because of ourselves), God works on our behalf through Jesus. The gospel meets us in our weakness, not our strength; in our dependence, not our independence. Prayer is a practice that takes the same form: weakness, dependence. It says, "I can't, so, God, you must." Real prayer sings its melody over the gospel's chord progressions. The gospel and prayer form one song whose refrain is "Not I, but Christ" (Gal. 2:20).

So if the gospel really is the power of God, prayer must work.

My hope is that *Before We Gather* creates a habit in you and your church that carries on well past the last devotion. My hope is that after my last devotion comes your first devotion. *Before We Gather* is a baton exchange in a long race. The first leg is over, and now that baton is being passed to you.

There is way more truth yet to break forth from the pages of Scripture. Read it. Study it. Pray it. And as you do so, I believe that the Spirit who breathes in it will breathe out of you more reflections to bring to your people, which will in turn energize yet more culture-changing prayer.

The baton is yours. And because Christ is yours, you're free to run.

# Acknowledgments

This book was written somewhere west of Ur. God said, "Go," but did not disclose the destination. I offer these acknowledgments on the other side of that journey, thankful for my new community, Church of the Cross—planted by God, loved by Jesus, sustained by the Spirit.

I'm especially thankful to the friends who took up their walking sticks beside me on my westward journey: David Hezlep, Kent Michael, Lee Scott, Joey Seales. Your companionship gave these pages life and humanity.

Two early readers and editors blessed me with wonderful comments and feedback: my talented mother, Brenda Hicks, and my gifted copastor, Jess Leslie. Raised by one, laboring beside the other—you both make me better.

Over the years, my ears have been sharpened to the finer frequencies of the gospel because of the friendship and theological mentorship of Jonathan Linebaugh. If the gospel resonates in these pages, it is in no small part because of your constancy in, fidelity to, and passion for the word of the cross.

Ryan Pazdur: thanks to you and the remarkable team at Zondervan for seeing value in this work for the church and for your precise and gracious editorial eye, along with Joshua Blunt—both of you made this clearer and more readable and heartfelt. Andrew Wolgemuth: prompt, personable, professional, genuinely kind, sincerely encouraging—thank you for helping me execute, hone, and present my ideas.

I want to give a shout-out to the gifted Birmingham worship leaders who helped me decide on a title and cover and, even more, gave me the confidence that this was a resource worth producing: Joel Burks, Annie Lee, Jess Leslie, Jeremy Moore, Savannah O'Rear, Lauren Starnes. Our city is in good shape because you are here.

I praise God for the church communities that mark my journey, where all the kinds of transformative prayer written about in this book happened: Waiʻalae Baptist Church (Honolulu, HI); First Baptist Church of Orange (Orange, CA); Rocky Mountain Presbyterian Church (Westminster, CO); Cherry Creek Presbyterian Church (Greenwood Village, CO); Coral Ridge Presbyterian Church (Fort Lauderdale, FL); Cathedral Church of the Advent (Birmingham, AL); Church of the Cross (Birmingham, AL). I would be lost without the local church.

Joel, Jesse, Brody, and Bronwyn: you four are my joy and inspiration. You have been God's instruments of greatest blessing, and I'm proud of the worshipers you are becoming. On September 13, 2020, God spoke clearly to me about all four of you as a preacher was reading Exodus 14:13. When life gets hard, ask me about that moment. I'll quote his exact words to you.

Abby: where would I be without you? You are faithful, steadfast, and selfless. You never cease to support and comfort, and you seem to be an endless well of giving. I know Christ's love best because of you. Thank you for your love and support.

# Topic Index

**Abraham**
    *15. The Antidote to Spiritual Amnesia*
**absence (of God)**
    *5. Where Did You Go, God?*
**abuse**
    *43. Good Old-Fashioned Submission*
    *44. A Safe Space*
**adoption**
    *14. Come, Holy Spirit*
**advocacy**
    *29. Christ Ascended*
**affections**
    *10. Worshiping God versus Worshiping Worship*
    *37. Shalom Worship*
    *38. Bezalel and Oholiab*
**African American worship tradition**
    *33. Lamentation as Praise*
**amnesia**
    *15. The Antidote to Spiritual Amnesia*
**angels**
    *1. Learning How to Pray*
    *35. More Than We Can See*
**anxiety**
    *5. Where Did You Go, God?*
    *13. Worshiping before the Nations*
    *36. God-Fearing*
    *51. Over the Chaos*
**art**
    *38. Bezalel and Oholiab*
**artistry**
    *38. Bezalel and Oholiab*
**attack**
    *9. Worship as Wait Training*
    *13. Worshiping before the Nations*

**baptism**
    *34. The Goal of Redemption*
    *45. Working Backward from the End*
**barrenness**
    *46. The Wilderness of Worship*
**battle**
    *26. Two More in the Battle*

**beholding**
    *31. The Spillover*
**betrayal**
    *2. Bring Your Burdens On In*
**Bible**
    *8. The Living and Active Word*
**black worship tradition**
    *33. Lamentation as Praise*
**blessing**
    *49. Easily Blessed*
**body**
    *37. Shalom Worship*
**bondage**
    *34. The Goal of Redemption*
**brokenness**
    *44. A Safe Space*
**bronze serpent**
    *11. Clear Glass, Not Stained Glass*
**burdens**
    *2. Bring Your Burdens On In*
**burnout**
    *18. Our Sacrifice of Praise*
**burnt offering**
    *29. Christ Ascended*

**chaos**
    *51. Over the Chaos*
**children**
    *28. Worship as Confrontation*
**Christ,** *see* **Jesus**
**Christian Calendar**
    *30. Jesus Time*
**Christmas**
    *37. Shalom Worship*
**church**
    body of Christ
        *12. The Lord Is My Song*
    universal
        *35. More Than We Can See*
**church calendar**
    *30. Jesus Time*
**comfort**
    *5. Where Did You Go, God?*

44. A Safe Space

**communion**
   3. The Worship of Our Ears
   24. Worship as Remembrance
   45. Working Backward from the End
   47. Worshiping "Before the Gods"
   50. So You Want to Encounter Jesus

**confession**
   4. On Being a Worthy Worshiper
   15. The Antidote to Spiritual Amnesia
   32. Always Repenting
   42. Beyond Us and Them
   48. Digging for His Presence
   52. What Qualifies Us to Serve

**consumerism**
   49. Easily Blessed

**control**
   43. Good Old-Fashioned Submission

**creation**
   22. The Day of the Lord
   38. Bezalel and Oholiab

**cross**
   3. The Worship of Our Ears
   5. Where Did You Go, God?
   11. Clear Glass, Not Stained Glass
   24. Worship as Remembrance

**David**
   46. The Wilderness of Worship

**day of the Lord**
   22. The Day of the Lord

**death**
   7. Worship That Makes Dead Things
     Alive

**deconstruction**
   7. Worship That Makes Dead Things
     Alive

**depression**
   5. Where Did You Go, God?

**desire**
   21. The Unbudding Fig Tree

**despair**
   7. Worship That Makes Dead Things
     Alive

**discipline**
   21. The Unbudding Fig Tree

**diversity**
   45. Working Backward from the End

**doubt**
   6. Finding True Reality

**dryness**
   5. Where Did You Go, God?
   18. Our Sacrifice of Praise
   31. The Spillover

**edification**
   49. Easily Blessed

**emotions**
   10. Worshiping God versus Worshiping
     Worship
   21. The Unbudding Fig Tree
   31. The Spillover
   37. Shalom Worship

**empathy**
   2. Bring Your Burdens On In

**encounter**
   50. So You Want to Encounter Jesus

**enemies**
   13. Worshiping before the Nations
   15. The Antidote to Spiritual Amnesia
   48. Digging for His Presence

**equality**
   45. Working Backward from the End

**ethics**
   42. Beyond Us and Them

**Eucharist**, *see* **communion**

**evangelism**
   13. Worshiping before the Nations
   17. When "Us versus Them" Becomes
     "We"
   34. The Goal of Redemption
   47. Worshiping "Before the Gods"

**evangelistic worship**
   47. Worshiping "Before the Gods"

**Exodus**
   24. Worship as Remembrance
   34. The Goal of Redemption

**failure**
   52. What Qualifies Us to Serve

**favoritism**
   17. When "Us versus Them" Becomes
     "We"

**fear**
   19. The Face of God
   36. God-Fearing

**feelings**
    10. *Worshiping God versus Worshiping Worship*
    21. *The Unbudding Fig Tree*
    31. *The Spillover*
    48. *Digging for His Presence*
**flesh**
    4. *On Being a Worthy Worshiper*
    15. *The Antidote to Spiritual Amnesia*
**forgetfulness**
    15. *The Antidote to Spiritual Amnesia*
**forgiveness**
    1. *Learning How to Pray*
    39. *Hearing Aids for the Gospel*
**formation**
    9. *Worship as Wait Training*
**fruit of the Spirit**
    38. *Bezalel and Oholiab*
    49. *Easily Blessed*

**glory**
    13. *Worshiping before the Nations*
    19. *The Face of God*
    27. *Glory*
**God**
    absence of
        5. *Where Did You Go, God?*
    discipline of
        21. *The Unbudding Fig Tree*
    existence of
        6. *Finding True Reality*
    face of
        19. *The Face of God*
    Father
        25. *The (Not So) Ordinary Work of the Holy Spirit*
    goodness of
        6. *Finding True Reality*
    "I Am"
        30. *Jesus Time*
    image of
        45. *Working Backward from the End*
    intimacy with
        1. *Learning How to Pray*
        27. *Glory*
        40. *You're Really Getting Married*
        42. *Beyond Us and Them*
    knowing
        31. *The Spillover*

    mercy of
        45. *Working Backward from the End*
        46. *The Wilderness of Worship*
    name of
        30. *Jesus Time*
    presence of
        2. *Bring Your Burdens On In*
        14. *Come, Holy Spirit*
        18. *Our Sacrifice of Praise*
        19. *The Face of God*
        48. *Digging for His Presence*
        50. *So You Want to Encounter Jesus*
    wrath of
        48. *Digging for His Presence*
**going through the motions**
    3. *The Worship of Our Ears*
**gospel**
    39. *Hearing Aids for the Gospel*
**Great Commandment**
    31. *The Spillover*

**Habakkuk**
    21. *The Unbudding Fig Tree*
**hardness of heart**
    48. *Digging for His Presence*
**hardship**
    13. *Worshiping before the Nations*
**head and heart together**
    31. *The Spillover*
**healing**
    11. *Clear Glass, Not Stained Glass*
**heart-centered worship**
    3. *The Worship of Our Ears*
**heaven**
    1. *Learning How to Pray*
    16. *The New Song*
    22. *The Day of the Lord*
    35. *More Than We Can See*
**heavenly worship**
    35. *More Than We Can See*
    45. *Working Backward from the End*
**holiness**
    4. *On Being a Worthy Worshiper*
**Holy Spirit**
    general entries
        3. *The Worship of Our Ears*
        7. *Worship That Makes Dead Things Alive*
        15. *The Antidote to Spiritual Amnesia*

16. *The New Song*
24. *Worship as Remembrance*
25. *The (Not So) Ordinary Work of the Holy Spirit*

advocate
26. *Two More in the Battle*
29. *Christ Ascended*

filling of
14. *Come, Holy Spirit*
38. *Bezalel and Oholiab*

fruit of
38. *Bezalel and Oholiab*
49. *Easily Blessed*

presence of
14. *Come, Holy Spirit*

**hope**
5. *Where Did You Go, God?*
7. *Worship That Makes Dead Things Alive*
9. *Worship as Wait Training*
33. *Lamentation as Praise*

**horizontal (dimension of worship)**
38. *Bezalel and Oholiab*

**hospitality**
47. *Worshiping "Before the Gods"*

**humility**
43. *Good Old-Fashioned Submission*

**hunger**
20. *Why Worship Isn't Always Fun*

**"I Am" statements**
30. *Jesus Time*

**identity**
24. *Worship as Remembrance*
34. *The Goal of Redemption*

**idolatry**
10. *Worshiping God versus Worshiping Worship*
28. *Worship as Confrontation*
47. *Worshiping "Before the Gods"*

**image of God**
45. *Working Backward from the End*

**inadequacy**
52. *What Qualifies Us to Serve*

**incarnation**
4. *On Being a Worthy Worshiper*
38. *Bezalel and Oholiab*

**iniquity**
32. *Always Repenting*

**integrity**
52. *What Qualifies Us to Serve*

**intellect**
37. *Shalom Worship*

**intimacy with God**
1. *Learning How to Pray*
27. *Glory*
40. *You're Really Getting Married*
42. *Beyond Us and Them*

**invocation**
14. *Come, Holy Spirit*

**isolation**
46. *The Wilderness of Worship*

**Israelite worship**
30. *Jesus Time*

**Jesus**
advocate
26. *Two More in the Battle*
29. *Christ Ascended*

ascension
29. *Christ Ascended*

Author and Perfecter of faith
4. *On Being a Worthy Worshiper*

Bridegroom
40. *You're Really Getting Married*

cornerstone
44. *A Safe Space*

crucifixion
5. *Where Did You Go, God?*
11. *Clear Glass, Not Stained Glass*
24. *Worship as Remembrance*

Friend of Sinners
2. *Bring Your Burdens On In*

High Priest
3. *The Worship of Our Ears*

imitation of
18. *Our Sacrifice of Praise*

Immanuel
19. *The Face of God*

incarnation
4. *On Being a Worthy Worshiper*
38. *Bezalel and Oholiab*

King
1. *Learning How to Pray*

Lamb of God
16. *The New Song*
45. *Working Backward from the End*

*Light of the World*
    *44. A Safe Space*
*substitute*
    *1. Learning How to Pray*
*temptation of*
    *46. The Wilderness of Worship*
*union with*
    *40. You're Really Getting Married*
*Word*
    *8. The Living and Active Word*
    *44. A Safe Space*
*Worship Leader*
    *1. Learning How to Pray*

**Jewish feasts and festivals**
    *30. Jesus Time*
**Job**
    *33. Lamentation as Praise*
**John the Baptist**
    *46. The Wilderness of Worship*
**Joseph**
    *15. The Antidote to Spiritual Amnesia*
**joy**
    *31. The Spillover*
    *48. Digging for His Presence*
**judgment**
    *11. Clear Glass, Not Stained Glass*
    *19. The Face of God*
    *22. The Day of the Lord*
    *46. The Wilderness of Worship*
**justice**
    *13. Worshiping before the Nations*
    *41. Symbiotic Worship*
    *48. Digging for His Presence*

**kingdom of God**
    *1. Learning How to Pray*
    *28. Worship as Confrontation*

**lamentation**
    *5. Where Did You Go, God?*
    *33. Lamentation as Praise*
**law and gospel**
    *11. Clear Glass, Not Stained Glass*
**leadership**
    *52. What Qualifies Us to Serve*
**life, meaning of**
    *34. The Goal of Redemption*

**listening**
    *43. Good Old-Fashioned Submission*
**loneliness**
    *26. Two More in the Battle*
    *46. The Wilderness of Worship*
**Lord's Prayer**
    *1. Learning How to Pray*
**Lord's Supper,** *see* **communion**
**Luther, Martin**
    *32. Always Repenting*

**marriage**
    *40. You're Really Getting Married*
**maturity**
    *49. Easily Blessed*
**media**
    *10. Worshiping God versus Worshiping Worship*
**mercy**
    *11. Clear Glass, Not Stained Glass*
    *41. Symbiotic Worship*
**ministry**
    *38. Bezalel and Oholiab*
    *52. What Qualifies Us to Serve*
**miracles**
    *7. Worship That Makes Dead Things Alive*
**missional worship**
    *13. Worshiping before the Nations*
**mission(s)**
    *13. Worshiping before the Nations*
    *17. When "Us versus Them" Becomes "We"*
    *29. Christ Ascended*
**morality, morals**
    *42. Beyond Us and Them*
**Moses**
    *15. The Antidote to Spiritual Amnesia*
**multicultural worship**
    *45. Working Backward from the End*
**mutuality**
    *45. Working Backward from the End*

**new heavens, new earth**
    *22. The Day of the Lord*
**non-Christians**
    *17. When "Us versus Them" Becomes "We"*
    *47. Worshiping "Before the Gods"*

**Old Testament worship**
    *30. Jesus Time*
**ordinances,** *see* **sacraments**

**passion**
    *13. Worshiping before the Nations*
**pastoring**
    *52. What Qualifies Us to Serve*
**patience**
    *9. Worship as Wait Training*
**Paul, the apostle**
    *39. Hearing Aids for the Gospel*
**peace**
    *37. Shalom Worship*
    *51. Over the Chaos*
**physical expression**
    *37. Shalom Worship*
**pleasure**
    *48. Digging for His Presence*
**politics**
    *43. Good Old-Fashioned Submission*
**postures of worship**
    *3. The Worship of Our Ears*
**power**
    *43. Good Old-Fashioned Submission*
**praise**
    *33. Lamentation as Praise*
**prayer**
    *1. Learning How to Pray*
    *14. Come, Holy Spirit*
    *25. The (Not So) Ordinary Work of the Holy Spirit*
    *27. Glory*
**preaching**
    *3. The Worship of Our Ears*
    *50. So You Want to Encounter Jesus*
**presence of God**
    *2. Bring Your Burdens On In*
    *14. Come, Holy Spirit*
    *18. Our Sacrifice of Praise*
    *19. The Face of God*
    *48. Digging for His Presence*
    *50. So You Want to Encounter Jesus*
**prophecy**
    *7. Worship That Makes Dead Things Alive*
**protection**
    *48. Digging for His Presence*

**Psalms**
    *16. The New Song*
**purification**
    *4. On Being a Worthy Worshiper*

**qualifications**
    *52. What Qualifies Us to Serve*

**racism**
    *45. Working Backward from the End*
**reality**
    *6. Finding True Reality*
**reconciliation**
    *1. Learning How to Pray*
**redemption**
    *15. The Antidote to Spiritual Amnesia*
    *24. Worship as Remembrance*
    *34. The Goal of Redemption*
**Reformation**
    *32. Always Repenting*
**refuge**
    *44. A Safe Space*
**remembrance**
    *15. The Antidote to Spiritual Amnesia*
    *24. Worship as Remembrance*
**renewal**
    *46. The Wilderness of Worship*
**repentance**
    *10. Worshiping God versus Worshiping Worship*
    *11. Clear Glass, Not Stained Glass*
    *32. Always Repenting*
    *36. God-Fearing*
    *46. The Wilderness of Worship*
**rest**
    *22. The Day of the Lord*
**resurrection**
    *7. Worship That Makes Dead Things Alive*
    *50. So You Want to Encounter Jesus*
**rituals**
    *3. The Worship of Our Ears*

**sabbath**
    *22. The Day of the Lord*
**sacraments**
    *6. Finding True Reality*
    *45. Working Backward from the End*

**sacred-secular distinction**
    *23. Enter with Thanksgiving*
**sacrifice**
    *3. The Worship of Our Ears*
    *8. The Living and Active Word*
    *18. Our Sacrifice of Praise*
**sacrificial system**
    *8. The Living and Active Word*
**safety**
    *44. A Safe Space*
**saints**
    *1. Learning How to Pray*
    *35. More Than We Can See*
**Satan**
    *15. The Antidote to Spiritual Amnesia*
    *26. Two More in the Battle*
**satisfaction**
    *20. Why Worship Isn't Always Fun*
**Scripture**
    *8. The Living and Active Word*
    *51. Over the Chaos*
**security**
    *44. A Safe Space*
**selflessness**
    *18. Our Sacrifice of Praise*
**senses (five senses)**
    *3. The Worship of Our Ears*
    *38. Bezalel and Oholiab*
**sermons**
    *3. The Worship of Our Ears*
    *50. So You Want to Encounter Jesus*
**shalom**
    *37. Shalom Worship*
**shelter**
    *44. A Safe Space*
**sin**
    *17. When "Us versus Them" Becomes "We"*
    *32. Always Repenting*
    *52. What Qualifies Us to Serve*
**singing**
    *1. Learning How to Pray*
    *12. The Lord Is My Song*
    *16. The New Song*
    *50. So You Want to Encounter Jesus*
**social media**
    *3. The Worship of Our Ears*
**songs**
    *16. The New Song*

**songwriting**
    *16. The New Song*
    *21. The Unbudding Fig Tree*
    *42. Beyond Us and Them*
**Spirit-filled worship**
    *14. Come, Holy Spirit*
    *16. The New Song*
    *25. The (Not So) Ordinary Work of the Holy Spirit*
    *39. Hearing Aids for the Gospel*
    *49. Easily Blessed*
    *51. Over the Chaos*
**spiritual attack**
    *9. Worship as Wait Training*
    *13. Worshiping before the Nations*
**spiritual formation**
    *9. Worship as Wait Training*
**spiritual warfare**
    *1. Learning How to Pray*
    *26. Two More in the Battle*
**stories**
    *15. The Antidote to Spiritual Amnesia*
**storytelling**
    *15. The Antidote to Spiritual Amnesia*
**struggle**
    *6. Finding True Reality*
**submission**
    *43. Good Old-Fashioned Submission*
**suffering**
    *7. Worship That Makes Dead Things Alive*
    *9. Worship as Wait Training*
    *21. The Unbudding Fig Tree*
    *33. Lamentation as Praise*
**Sunday**
    *22. The Day of the Lord*

**technology**
    *10. Worshiping God versus Worshiping Worship*
    *38. Bezalel and Oholiab*
**temptation**
    *1. Learning How to Pray*
    *46. The Wilderness of Worship*
**thankfulness**
    *23. Enter with Thanksgiving*
    *49. Easily Blessed*
**thanksgiving**
    *23. Enter with Thanksgiving*

49. *Easily Blessed*

**time**
30. *Jesus Time*

**tradition**
22. *The Day of the Lord*

**trauma**
44. *A Safe Space*

**Trinity**
25. *The (Not So) Ordinary Work of the Holy Spirit*
26. *Two More in the Battle*
27. *Glory*
40. *You're Really Getting Married*

**Trinitarian worship**
25. *The (Not So) Ordinary Work of the Holy Spirit*
26. *Two More in the Battle*
27. *Glory*

**union**
40. *You're Really Getting Married*

**visions**
45. *Working Backward from the End*

**waiting**
9. *Worship as Wait Training*

**warfare**
1. *Learning How to Pray*
26. *Two More in the Battle*

**Watts, Isaac**
31. *The Spillover*

**whole-life worship**
12. *The Lord Is My Song*
23. *Enter with Thanksgiving*
32. *Always Repenting*
36. *God-Fearing*
41. *Symbiotic Worship*

**wilderness**
46. *The Wilderness of Worship*

**will**
37. *Shalom Worship*

**wounding**
44. *A Safe Space*

# Bible Index

In the following entries, **boldface** indicates
a principal devotional passage.

## GENESIS

| | |
|---|---|
| 1 | 38. Bezalel and Oholiab |
| 1:1–2 | 51. Over the Chaos |
| 1:2 | 22. The Day of the Lord |
| 1:3 | 8. The Living and Active Word |
| 1:27 | 40. You're Really Getting Married |
| 2:1–3 | 22. The Day of the Lord |
| 3:1 | 43. Good Old-Fashioned Submission |
| 3:7 | 22. The Day of the Lord |
| 3:8 | 15. The Antidote to Spiritual Amnesia; 22. The Day of the Lord |
| 12:3 | 13. Worshiping before the Nations |
| 32:22–32 | 46. The Wilderness of Worship |

## EXODUS

| | |
|---|---|
| 3:11–12 | 34. The Goal of Redemption |
| 3:13–14 | 30. Jesus Time |
| **31:1–11** | **38. Bezalel and Oholiab** |
| 33:17–23 | 19. The Face of God |

## LEVITICUS

| | |
|---|---|
| 11:44 | 4. On Being a Worthy Worshiper |

## NUMBERS

| | |
|---|---|
| 21:4–9 | 11. Clear Glass, Not Stained Glass |

## DEUTERONOMY

| | |
|---|---|
| 6:5 | 31. The Spillover |

## JOSHUA

| | |
|---|---|
| 5:6 | 46. The Wilderness of Worship |

## 1 SAMUEL

| | |
|---|---|
| 23:24 | 46. The Wilderness of Worship |

## 2 SAMUEL

| | |
|---|---|
| 12:7 | 42. Beyond Us and Them |

## 2 CHRONICLES

| | |
|---|---|
| 20:15 | 26. Two More in the Battle |

## PSALMS

| | |
|---|---|
| 1:2 | 20. Why Worship Isn't Always Fun |
| **2** | **43. Good Old-Fashioned Submission** |
| 5:9 | 17. When "Us versus Them" Becomes "We" |
| 9:3 | 48. Digging for His Presence |
| 10:7 | 17. When "Us versus Them" Becomes "We" |
| 14:1–3 | 17. When "Us versus Them" Becomes "We" |
| **15:1–5** | **4. On Being a Worthy Worshiper** |
| 16:1–2 | 4. On Being a Worthy Worshiper |
| 16:11 | 48. Digging for His Presence |
| 17:2 | 48. Digging for His Presence |
| 21:6 | 48. Digging for His Presence |
| 22:2 | 1. Learning How to Pray |
| 22:22 | 12. The Lord Is My Song |
| **27:1–6** | **44. A Safe Space** |
| 27:8 | 19. The Face of God |
| **29** | **51. Over the Chaos** |
| 31:20 | 48. Digging for His Presence |
| 33:3 | 16. The New Song |
| 34:8 | 18. Our Sacrifice of Praise |
| **34:8–14** | **36. God-Fearing** |
| 34:18 | 21. The Unbudding Fig Tree |
| 36:1 | 17. When "Us versus Them" Becomes "We" |
| 40:6–8 | **3. The Worship of Our Ears** |
| 40:3 | 16. The New Song |
| **42** | **5. Where Did You Go, God?** |

48        10. Worshiping God versus
          Worshiping Worship
51:1–13   52. What Qualifies Us to
          Serve
51:12     31. The Spillover
53:1–3    17. When "Us versus Them"
          Becomes "We"
55:22     2. Bring Your Burdens On In
62        9. Worship as Wait Training
66:5–7    24. Worship as Remembrance
73        6. Finding True Reality
73:28     18. Our Sacrifice of Praise
81:10     49. Easily Blessed
90:8      48. Digging for His Presence
95:1–2    23. Enter with Thanksgiving
96:1      16. The New Song
98:1      16. The New Song
100:2     48. Digging for His Presence
103:8     46. The Wilderness of Worship
105:1–6   15. The Antidote to Spiritual
          Amnesia
105:4     19. The Face of God;
          48. Digging for His Presence
106:8–13  15. The Antidote to Spiritual
          Amnesia
107       32. Always Repenting
108       13. Worshiping before the
          Nations
108:2     31. The Spillover
114:1–8   19. The Face of God
114:7     48. Digging for His Presence
115:1–8   28. Worship as Confrontation
118:1–14  12. The Lord Is My Song
119:103   20. Why Worship Isn't Always
          Fun
127:2     49. Easily Blessed
132:13    50. So You Want to Encounter
          Jesus
138:1–6   47. Worshiping "Before the
          Gods"
139:1–18  31. The Spillover
139:7–12  14. Come, Holy Spirit
139:13–23 42. Beyond Us and Them
140:3     17. When "Us versus Them"
          Becomes "We"
144:9     16. The New Song
147:15–18 8. The Living and Active Word
149       16. The New Song;
          33. Lamentation as Praise

149:1     16. The New Song
150       10. Worshiping God versus
          Worshiping Worship

PROVERBS
3:34      17. When "Us versus Them"
          Becomes "We"

ISAIAH
42:10     16. The New Song
53:5      37. Shalom Worship
57:5–8    48. Digging for His Presence
57:14–15  48. Digging for His Presence
61:1–2    50. So You Want to Encounter
          Jesus
62:4–5    40. You're Really Getting
          Married
66:12–14  37. Shalom Worship

JEREMIAH
3:1–5     40. You're Really Getting
          Married
17:9      39. Hearing Aids for the
          Gospel

EZEKIEL
16        40. You're Really Getting
          Married
37:1–10   7. Worship That Makes Dead
          Things Alive; 14. Come, Holy
          Spirit

HOSEA
4:15      40. You're Really Getting
          Married

JOEL
2:31      22. The Day of the Lord

AMOS
5:18–24   41. Symbiotic Worship; 22. The
          Day of the Lord

HABAKKUK
1–3       21. The Unbudding Fig Tree
3:17–19   21. The Unbudding Fig Tree

ZEPHANIAH
3:17      12. The Lord Is My Song

## MALACHI

3:3    22. The Day of the Lord

## MATTHEW

3:1–6    46. The Wilderness of Worship
3:13–17    14. Come, Holy Spirit
3:17    18. Our Sacrifice of Praise
4:1–11    46. The Wilderness of Worship
4:4    6. Finding True Reality
4:17    32. Always Repenting
**6:7–13**    **1. Learning How to Pray**
7:7–11    23. Enter with Thanksgiving
9:15    40. You're Really Getting Married
11:19    2. Bring Your Burdens On In
11:25    28. Worship as Confrontation
11:28–30    2. Bring Your Burdens On In
11:29    44. A Safe Space
13:31–32    28. Worship as Confrontation
16:24    5. Where Did You Go, God?
18:21–22    1. Learning How to Pray
19:14    28. Worship as Confrontation
20:28    19. The Face of God
21:42    44. A Safe Space
22:37    31. The Spillover
22:37–38    36. God-Fearing
25:1–13    40. You're Really Getting Married
27:46    5. Where Did You Go, God?

## MARK

1:11    14. Come, Holy Spirit
2:17    20. Why Worship Isn't Always Fun
10:45    19. The Face of God

## LUKE

1:46–56    44. A Safe Space
4:16    50. So You Want to Encounter Jesus
11:1    25. The (Not So) Ordinary Work of the Holy Spirit
24:13–32    50. So You Want to Encounter Jesus
24:30–32    14. Come, Holy Spirit

## JOHN

1:1    7. Worship That Makes Dead Things Alive; 8. The Living and Active Word
1:14    4. On Being a Worthy Worshiper; 38. Bezalel and Oholiab
1:14–18    19. The Face of God
**3:14**    **11. Clear Glass, Not Stained Glass**
3:17    19. The Face of God
6:4    30. Jesus Time
6:35    30. Jesus Time
**6:41–51**    **30. Jesus Time**
6:51    23. Enter with Thanksgiving
6:53–56    20. Why Worship Isn't Always Fun
7:2    30. Jesus Time
8:12    30. Jesus Time; 44. A Safe Space
8:28    11. Clear Glass, Not Stained Glass
8:58    30. Jesus Time
10:7–9    30. Jesus Time
11:25    30. Jesus Time
14:6    30. Jesus Time
14:17    24. Worship as Remembrance
15:1–5    30. Jesus Time
16:7    29. Christ Ascended
16:8    47. Worshiping "Before the Gods"
16:8–11    8. The Living and Active Word
**17**    **27. Glory**
19:16–30    11. Clear Glass, Not Stained Glass
19:30    29. Christ Ascended
20:1–18    22. The Day of the Lord
20:22–23    39. Hearing Aids for the Gospel

## ACTS

**1:6–11**    **29. Christ Ascended**
2:38–39    14. Come, Holy Spirit
4:11    44. A Safe Space
10:2–35    36. God-Fearing
20:7    22. The Day of the Lord

## ROMANS

2:4    10. Worshiping God versus Worshiping Worship
3    45. Working Backward from the End

| 3:9–18 | 17. When "Us versus Them" Becomes "We" |
| 5:8 | 50. So You Want to Encounter Jesus |
| 6:3–4 | 34. The Goal of Redemption |
| 7:19–21 | 15. The Antidote to Spiritual Amnesia |
| 8:9 | 14. Come, Holy Spirit |
| 8:9–11 | 24. Worship as Remembrance |
| 8:11 | 14. Come, Holy Spirit |
| 8:14–17 | 47. Worshiping "Before the Gods" |
| 8:15 | 34. The Goal of Redemption |
| 8:15–17 | 14. Come, Holy Spirit; 44. A Safe Space |
| 8:15–18 | 25. The (Not So) Ordinary Work of the Holy Spirit |
| 8:26 | 5. Where Did You Go, God?; 14. Come, Holy Spirit |
| 8:26–34 | 26. Two More in the Battle |
| 8:38–39 | 40. You're Really Getting Married |
| 11:36 | 30. Jesus Time |
| 12:1 | 12. The Lord Is My Song; 41. Symbiotic Worship |
| 12:5 | 12. The Lord Is My Song |

## 1 CORINTHIANS

| 2:2 | 1. Learning How to Pray; 3. The Worship of Our Ears |
| 2:6–16 | 8. The Living and Active Word |
| 2:12 | 12. The Lord Is My Song |
| 2:27 | 12. The Lord Is My Song |
| 4:7 | 49. Easily Blessed |
| 8:4 | 47. Worshiping "Before the Gods" |
| 10:1–4 | 34. The Goal of Redemption |
| 11:24–25 | 24. Worship as Remembrance |
| 12:13 | 14. Come, Holy Spirit |
| 14 | 44. A Safe Space |
| 14:20–25 | 13. Worshiping before the Nations |
| 14:23–25 | 47. Worshiping "Before the Gods" |
| 15:20–23 | 7. Worship That Makes Dead Things Alive; 38. Bezalel and Oholiab |
| 16:2 | 22. The Day of the Lord |

## 2 CORINTHIANS

| 3:18 | 19. The Face of God |
| 5:17 | 34. The Goal of Redemption |
| 5:21 | 19. The Face of God |

## GALATIANS

| 1:3–9 | 39. Hearing Aids for the Gospel |
| 4:4–7 | 34. The Goal of Redemption |
| 5:16–17 | 15. The Antidote to Spiritual Amnesia |
| 5:17–24 | 39. Hearing Aids for the Gospel |
| 5:22–23 | 49. Easily Blessed |

## EPHESIANS

| 1:13–14 | 14. Come, Holy Spirit |
| 2:14 | 42. Beyond Us and Them |
| 2:20 | 44. A Safe Space |
| 4:12 | 12. The Lord Is My Song; 52. What Qualifies Us to Serve |
| 5:18–19 | 16. The New Song |
| 5:18–20 | 49. Easily Blessed |
| 5:18–21 | 14. Come, Holy Spirit; 43. Good Old-Fashioned Submission |
| 6:17 | 8. The Living and Active Word |

## PHILIPPIANS

| 1:15–17 | 44. A Safe Space |
| 2:1–11 | 18. Our Sacrifice of Praise |
| 3:3 | 4. On Being a Worthy Worshiper |

## COLOSSIANS

| 1:20 | 37. Shalom Worship |
| 3:15 | 12. The Lord Is My Song |
| 3:16 | 49. Easily Blessed |
| 3:16–17 | 8. The Living and Active Word |

## 1 THESSALONIANS

| 5:16–18 | 49. Easily Blessed |

## 1 TIMOTHY

| 3:1–13 | 52. What Qualifies Us to Serve |

## TITUS

| 1:7–9 | 52. What Qualifies Us to Serve |

# HEBREWS

| | |
|---|---|
| 1:3 | 27. Glory |
| 2:12 | 1. Learning How to Pray; 12. The Lord Is My Song |
| **4:12–13** | 3. The Worship of Our Ears; **8. The Living and Active Word**; 42. Beyond Us and Them; 47. Worshiping "Before the Gods" |
| 4:14–16 | 10. Worshiping God versus Worshiping Worship |
| 6:4–5 | 18. Our Sacrifice of Praise |
| 6:19–20 | 29. Christ Ascended |
| 7:23–28 | 26. Two More in the Battle |
| 9:11–28 | 26. Two More in the Battle |
| 10 | 3. The Worship of Our Ears |
| 10:5–7 | 3. The Worship of Our Ears |
| 10:11–14 | 29. Christ Ascended |
| 10:25 | 34. The Goal of Redemption |
| 12:2 | 4. On Being a Worthy Worshiper; 5. Where Did You Go, God?; 45. Working Backward from the End |
| 12:22–24 | 35. More Than We Can See |

# JAMES

| | |
|---|---|
| 4:6 | 17. When "Us versus Them" Becomes "We" |
| 4:10 | 43. Good Old-Fashioned Submission |

# 1 PETER

| | |
|---|---|
| 1:16 | 4. On Being a Worthy Worshiper |
| 2:6–7 | 44. A Safe Space |
| 5:5 | 17. When "Us versus Them" Becomes "We" |

# 2 PETER

| | |
|---|---|
| 3:9 | 48. Digging for His Presence |

# REVELATION

| | |
|---|---|
| 1:10 | 22. The Day of the Lord |
| 5:9 | 16. The New Song |
| **7:9–12** | **35. More Than We Can See; 45. Working Backward from the End** |
| 14:3 | 16. The New Song |
| **19:6–9** | **40. You're Really Getting Married** |

# Christian Calendar Index

The following entries are arranged in chronological order, starting with Advent.

**Advent**

5. *Where Did You Go, God?*
8. *The Living and Active Word*
9. *Worship as Wait Training*
15. *The Antidote to Spiritual Amnesia*
17. *When "Us versus Them" Becomes "We"*
19. *The Face of God*
27. *Glory*
30. *Jesus Time*
33. *Lamentation as Praise*
37. *Shalom Worship*
38. *Bezalel and Oholiab*
40. *You're Really Getting Married*
45. *Working Backward from the End*
46. *The Wilderness of Worship*
47. *Worshiping "Before the Gods"*
48. *Digging for His Presence*
51. *Over the Chaos*

**Christmas**

4. *On Being a Worthy Worshiper*
8. *The Living and Active Word*
27. *Glory*
37. *Shalom Worship*
38. *Bezalel and Oholiab*
48. *Digging for His Presence*
49. *Easily Blessed*

**Epiphany**

4. *On Being a Worthy Worshiper*
10. *Worshiping God versus Worshiping Worship*
17. *When "Us versus Them" Becomes "We"*
19. *The Face of God*
27. *Glory*
31. *The Spillover*
42. *Beyond Us and Them*
44. *A Safe Space*
49. *Easily Blessed*

**Lent**

1. *Learning How to Pray*
2. *Bring Your Burdens On In*

3. *The Worship of Our Ears*
5. *Where Did You Go, God?*
9. *Worship as Wait Training*
15. *The Antidote to Spiritual Amnesia*
17. *When "Us versus Them" Becomes "We"*
21. *The Unbudding Fig Tree*
24. *Worship as Remembrance*
32. *Always Repenting*
36. *God-Fearing*
41. *Symbiotic Worship*
42. *Beyond Us and Them*
46. *The Wilderness of Worship*
47. *Worshiping "Before the Gods"*
48. *Digging for His Presence*
52. *What Qualifies Us to Serve*

**Holy Week**

11. *Clear Glass, Not Stained Glass*
24. *Worship as Remembrance*

**Maundy Thursday/Good Friday**

5. *Where Did You Go, God?*
24. *Worship as Remembrance*

**Easter**

7. *Worship That Makes Dead Things Alive*
22. *The Day of the Lord*
26. *Two More in the Battle*
28. *Worship as Confrontation*
43. *Good Old-Fashioned Submission*
50. *So You Want to Encounter Jesus*

**Ascension**

29. *Christ Ascended*

**Pentecost/Ordinary Time**

*general entries*

1. *Learning How to Pray*
3. *The Worship of Our Ears*
6. *Finding True Reality*
7. *Worship That Makes Dead Things Alive*
12. *The Lord Is My Song*
13. *Worshiping before the Nations*
14. *Come, Holy Spirit*

15. *The Antidote to Spiritual Amnesia*
16. *The New Song*
18. *Our Sacrifice of Praise*
19. *The Face of God*
20. *Why Worship Isn't Always Fun*
23. *Enter with Thanksgiving*
25. *The (Not So) Ordinary Work of the Holy Spirit*
26. *Two More in the Battle*
28. *Worship as Confrontation*
31. *The Spillover*
33. *Lamentation as Praise*
34. *The Goal of Redemption*
35. *More Than We Can See*
38. *Bezalel and Oholiab*
39. *Hearing Aids for the Gospel*
41. *Symbiotic Worship*
45. *Working Backward from the End*
49. *Easily Blessed*
51. *Over the Chaos*

*Trinity*
25. *The (Not So) Ordinary Work of the Holy Spirit*
26. *Two More in the Battle*
27. *Glory*
40. *You're Really Getting Married*

*Reformation Day*
32. *Always Repenting*

*All Saints' Day*
1. *Learning How to Pray*
35. *More Than We Can See*

*Christ the King*
1. *Learning How to Pray*
12. *The Lord Is My Song*
23. *Enter with Thanksgiving*
26. *Two More in the Battle*
30. *Jesus Time*
31. *The Spillover*
43. *Good Old-Fashioned Submission*
44. *A Safe Space*
45. *Working Backward from the End*
50. *So You Want to Encounter Jesus*

# Worship Pastor Theme Index

The following entries are arranged in the order in which the themes appear in *The Worship Pastor.*

**Church Lover**

17. *When "Us versus Them" Becomes "We"*
26. *Two More in the Battle*
40. *You're Really Getting Married*
42. *Beyond Us and Them*

**Corporate Mystic**

3. *The Worship of Our Ears*
12. *The Lord Is My Song*
14. *Come, Holy Spirit*
16. *The New Song*
18. *Our Sacrifice of Praise*
19. *The Face of God*
24. *Worship as Remembrance*
27. *Glory*
31. *The Spillover*
36. *God-Fearing*
48. *Digging for His Presence*
50. *So You Want to Encounter Jesus*
51. *Over the Chaos*

**Doxological Philosopher**

12. *The Lord Is My Song*
14. *Come, Holy Spirit*
17. *When "Us versus Them" Becomes "We"*
23. *Enter with Thanksgiving*
37. *Shalom Worship*
41. *Symbiotic Worship*
42. *Beyond Us and Them*

**Disciple Maker**

12. *The Lord Is My Song*
16. *The New Song*
39. *Hearing Aids for the Gospel*
49. *Easily Blessed*

**Prayer Leader**

1. *Learning How to Pray*
16. *The New Song*
25. *The (Not So) Ordinary Work of the Holy Spirit*

**Theological Dietician**

7. *Worship That Makes Dead Things Alive*

21. *The Unbudding Fig Tree*
23. *Enter with Thanksgiving*
36. *God-Fearing*
39. *Hearing Aids for the Gospel*

**War General**

9. *Worship as Wait Training*
11. *Clear Glass, Not Stained Glass*
15. *The Antidote to Spiritual Amnesia*
26. *Two More in the Battle*
46. *The Wilderness of Worship*
48. *Digging for His Presence*

**Watchful Prophet**

5. *Where Did You Go, God?*
6. *Finding True Reality*
7. *Worship That Makes Dead Things Alive*
8. *The Living and Active Word*
9. *Worship as Wait Training*
10. *Worshiping God versus Worshiping Worship*
11. *Clear Glass, Not Stained Glass*
13. *Worshiping before the Nations*
20. *Why Worship Isn't Always Fun*
22. *The Day of the Lord*
28. *Worship as Confrontation*
33. *Lamentation as Praise*
35. *More Than We Can See*
41. *Symbiotic Worship*
43. *Good Old-Fashioned Submission*
45. *Working Backward from the End*
48. *Digging for His Presence*
51. *Over the Chaos*

**Missionary**

13. *Worshiping before the Nations*
17. *When "Us versus Them" Becomes "We"*
29. *Christ Ascended*
34. *The Goal of Redemption*
42. *Beyond Us and Them*
47. *Worshiping "Before the Gods"*

**Artist Chaplain**

38. *Bezalel and Oholiab*

**Caregiver**

2. Bring Your Burdens On In
5. Where Did You Go, God?
26. Two More in the Battle
44. A Safe Space
48. Digging for His Presence

**Mortician**

5. Where Did You Go, God?
7. Worship That Makes Dead Things Alive
22. The Day of the Lord
24. Worship as Remembrance
33. Lamentation as Praise
35. More Than We Can See
45. Working Backward from the End

**Emotional Shepherd**

8. The Living and Active Word
9. Worship as Wait Training
10. Worshiping God versus Worshiping Worship
16. The New Song
21. The Unbudding Fig Tree
31. The Spillover
37. Shalom Worship
39. Hearing Aids for the Gospel
41. Symbiotic Worship
48. Digging for His Presence

**Liturgical Architect**

7. Worship That Makes Dead Things Alive
15. The Antidote to Spiritual Amnesia
29. Christ Ascended
30. Jesus Time

32. Always Repenting
39. Hearing Aids for the Gospel
41. Symbiotic Worship
48. Digging for His Presence
51. Over the Chaos

**Curator**

1. Learning How to Pray
6. Finding True Reality
7. Worship That Makes Dead Things Alive
12. The Lord Is My Song
15. The Antidote to Spiritual Amnesia
16. The New Song
25. The (Not So) Ordinary Work of the Holy Spirit
32. Always Repenting
45. Working Backward from the End
46. The Wilderness of Worship
51. Over the Chaos

**Tour Guide**

general entries
7. Worship That Makes Dead Things Alive
15. The Antidote to Spiritual Amnesia
28. Worship as Confrontation
32. Always Repenting
35. More Than We Can See
41. Symbiotic Worship
46. The Wilderness of Worship
failure
4. On Being a Worthy Worshiper
40. You're Really Getting Married
52. What Qualifies Us to Serve